D1739990

AFTER LIVING ALL his life in India, and being very much a home keeping person, Nirad C Chaudhuri went abroad for the first time at the age of fifty-seven. It was a brief, five weeks visit to England.

In that short space of time he saw more paintings and works of art, more plays, fine buildings, gardens and beautiful landscapes; heard more poetry and music; ate and drank better; and altogether had a more exciting and interesting time than all the rest of his life.

A PASSAGE TO ENGLAND is a vivid account of his delightful voyage of discovery. It is vintage Nirad Chaudhuri. He has written with 'freedom to be himself', without any obligation of being informative, edifying, hortatory, or even serious. In his own words, "This means that it is only the sensations (to be carefully distinguished from emotions) of what I experienced which furnish the material of this book. And I know that only such a treatment can justify the writing of the account; any other would be both foolish and conceited."

NIRAD C CHAUDHURI was born in Kishorganj in Bengal, and lived in Delhi before settling down in Oxford in 1970, a place he fell in love with at first sight'. He is married to Amiya, also an author.

By the Same Author
in
Orient Paperbacks

Scholar Extraordinary:
The Life of F. Max Muller
To Live or Not to Live

A PASSAGE TO ENGLAND

NIRAD C. CHAUDHURI

ORIENT PAPERBACKS
A Division of Vision Books Pvt. Ltd.
New Delhi • Bombay

ISBN-81-222-0112-1

1st Published in Orient Paperbacks 1971
6th Printing 1982
This new edition 1994

A Passage to England

© Nirad C. Chaudhuri

Cover Design by Vision Studio

Published by
Orient Paperbacks
(A Division of Vision Books Pvt. Ltd.)
Madarsa Road, Kashmere Gate, Delhi - 110 006

Printed in India at
Cambridge Press, Delhi - 110 006

Cover Printed at
Ravindra Printing Press, Delhi-110 006

Contents

PART IV
STATE OF THE NATION

ACKNOWLEDGEMENTS

WHATEVER MAY BE THOUGHT of the intelligence and even character of a man who writes a book about a country after seeing it for only five weeks, that can make no difference to my gratitude to those who made the experience possible. My thanks are due in the first instance to the British Broadcasting Corporation (in my eye a small number of men and not an impersonal institution) for having thought of inviting me to see England and write a few talks for its Overseas Service. This, I was told, was an experiment, and a very risky one it was, for they were backing a completely dark horse. Even after the delivery of the talks and the broadcasts I had no means of knowing whether I had also run. For me personally, however, it was a windfall.

I have also to thank the B.B.C. for permission to incorporate the material of the broadcasts in this book and to adopt for it the title they gave to the series.

After that I would record my gratitude to the British Council (again a small number of individuals) for their hospitality to me. That it is the purpose of the Council to help visitors is no explanation of what I received. The efficiency of the arrangements and their smooth working could be anticipated, but not the personal touch. Of course, I too had a number, IND 320/38, and I also saw a chart on which the movements of a number of exotic birds of passage were plotted. But that was behind the scenes, where I had no right to pry. What I was made to feel was that I was in the hands of friends, and not of an organization. If there is still any disposition among the English people to sharpen their wits on the Council, it should be given up. I shall always think of those who looked after me on behalf of the B.B.C. and the British Council as my friends.

Next, I have to thank the French Foreign Office and the French Embassy in Delhi for offering me their hospitality in Paris. I have not been able to include an account of my experiences there in this book, but the scattered references that occur in it will, I hope, show that my visit to France was as great a romance as my stay in England.

I am obliged to *The Statesman* (Calcutta and Delhi) and *The Illustrated Weekly of India* (Bombay) for allowing me to make use of a number of articles on my Western visit which I wrote for them. I am also indebted to three friends and my son for permission to quote from their letters, and to the following for permission to make citations: The Clarendon Press, Oxford, for the quotation from Robert Bridges' *The Testament of Beauty* and Augener Limited for the musical quotation from Schumann: *Op. 9,* edited by X. Scharwenka.

Last of all, I am grateful to my publishers, in this instance as in the case of my first book, for having taken care of the English of a man who has learnt the language only from his Bengali teachers and from books.

NIRAD C. CHAUDHURI

PLEA FOR THE BOOK

AFTER LIVING ALL MY life in my own country, India, and being very much of a home-keeping person even there, I went abroad for the first time at the age of fifty-seven. It was in the spring of 1955 that I paid a short visit of five weeks to England, rounding it off with two weeks in Paris and one in Rome. As it happened, on the day I boarded the aeroplane for England, I was exactly 2,992 weeks old, and I spent eight weeks outside my country, thus completing a round three-thousand-week span by the time I returned to Delhi, where I live.

The point of giving these figures lies in the range and intensity of the experiences I went through in these eight weeks. In that short space of time I saw more paintings, statues, and works of art in general, more plays, fine buildings, gardens, and beautiful landscapes; heard more poetry and music; ate and drank better; and altogether had a more exciting and interesting time than in all the rest of my life. Hardly less important is the fact that among all these things were a great many that I had longed to see since my boyhood.

Naturally, I was in high spirits, and to begin with I wanted to share them with my countrymen. So I published one or two articles in the Indian Press. The result was, however, discouraging and even humiliating for me. It seemed as if I had given deep offence to a large number of my patriotic fellow-Indians by an indiscreet enthusiasm. There was some bad-tempered comment, not too elegantly put, on my performance. I was even called pro-British, which is one of the worst terms of abuse in contemporary India. As politics, in the strict sense of the word, are going to be excluded from the book, I shall not try to substantiate this statement. But I should like the English people to take my word for it that there is no greater myth than the much-talked-about Indo-British friendship since 1947.

But I am grateful to my critics for having released me from any obligation to be informative, edifying, hortatory, or even serious and for giving me the freedom to be myself in whatever I should write about my visit. This means that it is only the sensations (to be carefully distinguished from emotions) of what I experienced which will furnish the material of this book. And I know that only such a treatment can justify the writing of the account; any other would be both foolish and conceited.

Perhaps the book would have been nearer to what it aims to be if it could have been written down at the time of the visit. Even if I had kept only a diary, extracts from it would have embodied much more immediacy of feeling. But both were quite impossible. I had neither the time, nor in fact the inclination. I have never, at any time of my life, kept notes of my experiences, nor even of my reading. That, to my thinking, weakens experiencing, and converts living into something like cramming for examinations or writing a doctoral thesis. Besides, when abroad, I was very much in the state described by Wordsworth. What I was seeing was to me:

> An appetite; a feeling and a love,
> That had no need of a remoter charm,
> By thought supplied, nor any interest
> Unborrowed from the eye.

So, when my new English friends asked me what I was thinking of it all, I replied at times, 'I am only carrying back exposed films. They will have to be developed before I can say anything.' In the months that followed they were developed, and I can only hope that the resulting pictures are sharp.

But the process of recalling the sensations in tranquillity was bound to set in motion the parallel and rival process of thinking as well, which could not be de-intellectualized beyond the point of being transformed into musing. So I fear that in spite of my best efforts to decant the ratiocinative sediment some of it remains in the final product and cannot be separated. If for this reason the book tastes like muddy port, I have to take the blame.

However, one good may be claimed to have come out of the prolonged brooding. I have become fully aware of what my senses were dealing with, and also seen that they were working within very strict limits. They were fastening on certain things, and totally refusing to admit others. If I were to state what these limits were there would be less surprise over the omissions and inclusions in my account than if I left the reader without an explanation. That would also lessen the presumption that lies in trying to write even an impressionistic account after seeing a country for only five weeks.

What my senses were dealing with and striving hard to grasp was the reality I would call Timeless England, which I was seeing for the first time, and which I was inevitably led to set against the Timeless India in which I had been steeped all my life. Any acuity of the senses that I developed when abroad was due, not to any innate perceptivity, but to the impact of one big and unfamiliar reality on another equally big though familiar. That is why in this account of England India will be found to be walking in freely. I could not define my sensations about the new country without placing them against those about the only country known to me. In fact, I do not think I had any conscious theory at all: my senses worked below the conscious level in such a manner that one-half of my perception of England was the perception of something *not-India*. I saw things there in doublets—there were the things which were positively English, but there were also their shadows cast in a dark mass under the light from India. If I had stayed longer and got even partially acclimatized to my new surroundings, the sense of contrast would have been weakened, but with it my perception would also have become less vivid.

Of course, my mind was not a clean slate. On the contrary, it was burdened with an enormous load of book-derived notions, which were of two kinds. My earlier, and as I believe truer, ideas of England were all acquired from literature, history, and geography. Accumulated since childhood, these ideas, so far as they went, had built up a fairly comprehensive and homogeneous picture of the country and its people. On this was superimposed all the news of their political, social, and economic troubles that had been broadcast to the world in the previous forty years or so. There is no other nation which has shown greater energy in publicizing its ills, or done this more effectively. This volubility in hypochondria has helped the formation throughout the world, and more especially in the hostile East, of the conception of a people stricken incurably by decadence, who have become permanently sick. Although with me this picture of valetudinarianism did not wholly succeed in effacing the recollection of Merry England, I too was not immune to the idea of decay. So I did have some apprehension of seeing a faded and mouldy existence, and a distracted and weary people, leading a courageous but rather drab life.

This England of the public prints; of shattering jargon, deadening cliches, and pseudo-smart journalese, will be absent from the book. I saw very little of it. My hosts did indeed try to show me this aspect of English life. They were intellectuals, who had Old England in the blood and the Welfare State on the brain. They wanted me to take a balanced view of things, to be properly shared between their poetry and their economics. But my heart was not in it. Fortunately, for the greater part of my stay in England there was the newspaper strike, and I was spared even the duty of having to read about the public existence of the English people. Therefore, it is with their private life as a nation that my record will be almost exclusively concerned.

Certainly a great many changes have come over this private existence as well, some for the worse and others for the better. I was told about them, and more especially about the changes seen since the war. In print one is, of course, always reading about the transformations which are making England different, almost unrecognizable as Old England. But I could not read or listen to all this with full conviction. I asked myself, 'Are the changes so very thoroughgoing? Why, to me it looks very much like what I expected it to be, from reading and imagining.' To be frank, I thought today's England was very much like the England of history and perfectly consistent with it. I noticed the continuity more than the break.

There might be a way of reconciling these opposed views. Living through the changes, Englishmen would notice them more, overlooking the basic structure and functioning of their national existence, while to a newcomer like me the fundamentals would be more conspicuous than the overtones. A young man who sees a girl every day is given to judging her appearance very much by her freckles, sunburn, dresses, make-up, ways of doing her hair, and other externals. Also, in our times there is an over-emphasis on these things. Indeed, judging by the advertisements in the popular press, one would think that there was no such thing as a human soul, or for that matter even body, and that personality was an assemblage of cosmetics, underclothing, overclothing, and the like. In the same way, in regard to national life the newspapers and public discussion unduly magnify the changes, for their own functioning depends on this. As a result there grows up the habit of overlooking or underestimating the permanent form and spirit of a society.

Besides, there is something in the outlook of an Englishman which makes him feel the wholeness of a thing as the mere sum of its states and attributes for the time being. Nearly thirty years ago I read in a small book by Julien Benda that for the English people there exists the idea of a red rose, a white rose, a rose in bud, a rose in full bloom, but as for the idea of a rose which is neither red, nor white, nor in bud, nor in full bloom, the *abstract* idea of a rose, that is something which these Lockes and John Stuart Mills have the greatest difficulty in conceiving. Benda concluded, 'I have been told about a dog which recognized its master standing, but when he lay down barked at him, refusing to abstract the common element in these two objects. You may be sure that it was an English dog.'

That is perhaps why there was such a furore over the changes in the Prayer Book, and why many people think that the revisions have destroyed the character of the English Bible. This associationism, this habit of identifying the general wholly with its particular details, is very strange in a people who have shown themselves so capable of adapting themselves to new circumstances, who have in the last three hundred years averted bloody revolutions by carrying out imperceptible ones, who acquired an empire without seeming to notice it, who have lost it without being very sorry, who have always been saying that in what they have improved they have never been wholly new and in what they have retained never wholly obsolete. Possibly the lamentation over the changes is only talk, or even a mannerism, but even so it is a paradox.

This harping on the changes reminded me of Caroline Bingley's remark about Elizabeth Bennet: 'How very ill Eliza Bennet looks this morning, Mr. Darcy. I never in my life saw anyone so much altered as she is since the winter. She is grown so brown and coarse! Louisa and I were agreeing that we should not have known her again.' I also felt like replying, as the undeclared lover Darcy actually did, that I perceived no other alteration than her being rather tanned—no miraculous consequence of travelling in the summer.

I would make it clear, however, that I do not deny that far reaching changes have taken place, and possibly more are yet to be seen. But I cannot accept the usual appraisement of their effect on the historical personality of the English people. There is such a thing as stability in motion, immutability in flux. The more I think about the matter, the more convinced do I feel that nations acquire a sort of monumentality in their passage through history. Since to exist is to change, nothing can hope to remain always the same, but I cannot believe that such changes destroy the once formed personality of a people or civilization, or alter their basic character.

I see this in my own country. There is a permanent and basic India which is breaking all the changes it is going through into conformity with its essential nature. This India remains capable of dealing in its own way and time, not only with the chattering fidgetiness of the anglicized upper middle class, which is no worse than an attack of migraine, but even with the much more dangerously infective lower middle-class sullage which is being washed into the Jumna and the Ganges from the Thames and the Hudson, poor rivers all!

England too has acquired the same kind of monumentality and cannot be made unrecognizable as her historic self by any transformations that have already taken place or will in the future, however far-reaching they might be, in appearance or reality.

But the permanent face of India and the permanent face of England are different, they wear different looks. Time has made the face of my country stark, chastened, and sad, and it remains so in spite of the lipstick that is being put on it by the hand of the spiritual half-castes. The face of England remains smiling. When I was in England I felt this contrast, as well as the timelessness. If this book has any purpose more ambitious than the straightforward one of setting down a small number of impressions with some whimsical *obiter dicta*, it is the wish to convey a little of this feeling of permanence and antithesis.

And, finally, since another plea in defence of this plea is unthinkable, I apologize for its dogmatic and doctrinaire tone.

PART I

The English Scene

I

A WORLD OF ILLUSION

THERE IS A BELIEF in the West that we Hindus regard the world as an illusion. We do not, and indeed cannot, for the only idea of an after-life unquestioningly accepted by a Hindu—the unconscious assumption behind all that he does—is that he will be born again and again in the same old world and live in it virtually for eternity, with only short breaks for passage from one birth to another. What he is told beyond this by the philosophers is neither very intelligible nor attractive. It only assures him of the negation of everything he knows, an Absolute Nothing. A people who have learnt to believe in that way are not likely to be the persons most ready to dismiss the world as insubstantial.

But perhaps we give the nations of the West the impression of being indifferent to the world, by their standards, by exhibiting a marked lack of energy in meddling with our environment. This, however, is partly due to the climate, which makes us easygoing and indolent, not such bad things to be in the low latitudes. In equal measure it is to be set down to a subconscious philosophy which is not less logical than the consciously formulated philosophy of the Vedanta. We simply act in the spirit of the saying that you cannot have your cake and eat it.

Now, to enjoy the world is to exploit it, and to exploit it is to reduce its substance. It is natural in Christian Occidentals to indulge this propensity. Their religion teaches them to put their faith in a transcendental world and to live in anticipation of it, in the hope of leading an eternal though disembodied existence after the destruction of the material universe. Even those who have forgotten their Christian eschatology have kept up the habit of mind fostered by it. So they can use up the material world, bear to see all its iron, coal and oil being exhausted, and even take pride in squandering the cosmos with rakish self-indulgence. But we who believe in rebirth have to consider the unborn, who will be ourselves. Therefore we look upon the world as a property entailed in our favour for all time, and prefer to let it lie fallow for fear of disinheriting ourselves.

I think this is also at the bottom of the Hindu habit of hoarding money and the Hindu moral commandment: 'Thou shalt not spend more than a quarter of thine income.' We deny ourselves every comfort, contemptuously rejecting the Western notion of improving the standard of living, in order to lay by and leave a fortune at death, so that we may not be poor in future births. We cannot indeed guarantee that we shall inherit our own wealth, but by making the saving habit universal we can at least ensure that everyone will come into some kind of inheritance. This is our way of creating a Welfare State.

So I am inclined to think that this notion that a Hindu considers the world to be an illusion, in so far as it has not been foisted on us by Vedantizing Occidentals, is only an antidote devised by the Hindu moralists to cure us of our desperate clinging to things mundane.

But once in my life, though a Hindu, I did have a feeling that the world was a phantom. That was when I was in England. Yet it had not begun so. From the morning when we had taken off from Rome, all Europe was unfolding below me like a map, an enormous relief map. One of the advantages of air travel is that it simplifies a man's introduction to a new country by giving him a bird's-eye view of it, presenting it very much as it exists in a geography book.

As the aeroplane flew over Rome the city's well-known landmarks flashed past one after another: the Pyramid of Cestius, the Colosseum, the Forum, the Capitol, the Piazza del Popolo, the Pincio, the Villa Borghese, St Peter's. I could even see the Ponte Milvio, where the Cross had won its greatest secular victory, the only victory that was military. All these I could identify from map-knowledge.

A little later I saw a lake, which I took for Lake Trasimene, and I remarked to the fellow-passenger in the next seat, an

English accountant practising in Hong Kong, 'That is where the Romans fought a great battle,' meaning the disastrous one with Hannibal.

'Where two gods came to their aid?' he asked. Obviously he was thinking of Lake Regillus. I was corrected but at the same time felt delighted to find an English accountant practising in Hong Kong who remembered his Livy or at all events his *Lays of Ancient Rome*. But when on my way back I was staying in Rome, an Italian professor told me that Lake Regillus had dried up, and what I had seen must have been Lake Bolsena.

In spite of this mistake my knowledge of European geography on the whole stood the test of the air journey. I saw the Main and the Moselle winding into the Rhine just as they did on the large-scale maps I had at home, and thought, not of the battle of the Bulge for which I had procured them, but of the vineyards. I spotted the royal palace, the zoo, and the Palais de Justice,when we were passing over Brussels, and at the time of crossing the Channel between Ostend and Margate I found that corner of Kent looking exactly as it did in the atlas. The famous chalk cliffs did not stand out glimmering and vast, as Matthew Arnold had described, but seemed like white creases between the blue-grey sheet of the Channel and the mist-softened green expanse of Kent. And as we were coming down on London Airport I caught sight of Windsor Castle and Eton College Chapel, which I could recognize from the air. I thought it was a good omen that the first historic buildings to catch my eyes on my arrival in England should be these renowned symbols of English life.

But all this confidence vanished as soon as I landed on the ground, and bewilderment took its place. I had no previous idea that things which were so familiar to me from description and pictures, which I could still identify as objects in outline, could become so strange and different in their three dimensions, atmosphere and personality. As long as I remained in England a persistent trance-like effect never left me, and nothing seemed quite real, not even the human beings I was meeting. The only persons who appeared to be made of flesh and blood were the Englishmen I had known in India. All the rest glided like wraiths.

By a curious chance the first play I saw in London, which was also the first play on the public stage that I had seen in my life, strengthened the impression. It was *As You Like It* at the Old Vic, and shortly afterwards *The Magic Flute* at Sadler's Wells confirmed the spell. I daresay the large crowds of men and women I saw at these places had come to seek there the romance they could not find even in its most democratic standby, the cinema, but for me their own existence did not seem very different from what I saw on the stage. So, after coming back to London from Stratford-upon-Avon, I wrote to my family:

> 'As I roam about I still have a sense of the unreality of all that I am seeing, the light is different, the atmosphere is different, the smells, colours, and sounds are different. Even when I meet people, for example, when I met old Mr P— and Mrs P—, or Mr and Mrs H—, I wondered if I was not calling up in a strange and intolerably vivid dream something I had read about in an English novel. In one sense, England has not become more real to me than it was.'

One of my sons, all of whom have been brought up too carefully not to be capable of taking the healthy exercise of being disrespectful to their father, wrote thus to an American friend of his, after quoting the above passage: 'Father has lived too long in the world of books in regard to these places, don't you think so?'

He was not being very profound, though. A man who has lived too long in the world of books in regard to anything, be it landscape or love, in the sense of having formed a wholly imaginary and romanticized conception of what is described in them, does not project his mental picture to transform the reality, he complains and whimpers over the shattering of the dream. The sort of cobweb is always crumpled up by actual experience.

My wonder, so far as it had anything to do with books—and it had a good deal to do with them—was due to quite a different reason. I felt as I did partly because what I was seeing corresponded almost preternaturally to what I had read about in books, and yet was infinitely more solid, tangible, and therefore more over-powering to the senses. If an Englishman were to find the world described in *Alice in Wonderland* actually presenting itself to his eyes he would have had a feeling broadly resembling mine. In no case was the idea of England I had gained from books contradicted by anything I saw, it was on the contrary completed, and that is why I can no longer recover the original bookish idea. It has been absorbed by the reality of which it was an abstraction, like thawing ice in water.

English literature is the best guide for foreigners to the English scene because it is more closely the product of its geographical environment, more ecological, than any other literature I have read. I think English literature has gone farthest in fusing Nature and the spirit of man.

I was led to reassert this to myself by a remark made to me at Oxford. I was walking to my hotel from the railway station, when, catching sight of a line of low hills to the south, I asked my companion, 'Are those Cumnor Hills, and is Bablock Hythe in that direction?' He looked at me and put a counter-question, 'Are you thinking of Matthew Arnold?' When I replied, 'Yes', he observed, 'That is interesting, for I have been reading a book by an Indian who says that his countrymen come to England with too many literary associations in their mind and are consequently disappointed.'

'I am not disappointed,' was all that I said audibly, but my mental comment on this Indian was severe. It did not become an Indian, I thought, to air that kind of contempt for literature which came naturally to an English Barbarian, and to pretend that he was brought up on the *Pink 'Un* from childhood was even more unbecoming. But there were in the olden days in India a class of Indians trained to behave in that way by a class of Englishmen. An Englishman of this type resented our devotion to English literature as a sort of illicit attention to his wife, whom he himself was neglecting for his mistress, sport. Therefore he cast the Tenth Commandment in our teeth, tried to cure us of our literary-mindedness, and at the same time sneered at it. The Indians who lent themselves to this treatment and as a result acquired the anti-literary pose, came mostly from the very wealthy and princely classes, who, as Kipling put it, were bear-led by their English tutors.

As an Indian of the ordinary type I am not ashamed to say that if I am to be anything of an Englishman at all, I would rather be an imitation of Jeeves, the manservant, than of his gentleman master. We stand nowhere in regard to England if we give up things like literature. Neither the racehorse, nor cricket and football, nor even whisky, on which greater reliance is often placed, can be an adequate substitute. We cannot say as an Australian, New Zealander, or even American can say to his son, 'Go and see that manor or farm, for that is where your ancestors came from.' It is not for us to say that blood is thicker than water. The only ties felt in the heart that we can have with England are those created by things of the mind. The Englishmen who did their best to break those ties have lost the Indian Empire, and the Indians who allowed them to do so are the most bored or querulous set of foreigners who visit England.

II

MEETING THE THIRD DIMENSION

BUT THERE WAS ALSO something external behind this sense of unreality, and it was, of course, the combination of light and temperature. People from the tropics need a certain level of warmth inside and outside themselves to awaken their sense of actuality, and in its absence, if their faculties do not go into hibernation, they get a feeling as if they were in the castle of the Sleeping Beauty. This is so weirdly oppressive that many reduce their sensibility and observe even less in England than they do in their own countries.

The same effect is felt by the people of cold countries when it becomes unusually hot for them. At Oxford an English friend to whom I mentioned this impression of unreality immediately remarked, 'Mr Chaudhuri, we have the same kind of feeling just for a day or two in the summer, and that is where the phrase "midsummer madness" has come from.' I can well believe that, for on my return to Delhi even I was dazed as a result of the transition from 40°-60°F. to 85°-105°F. in about twenty-four hours.

The light on its part never appears like full daylight to us. To me it always seemed to be dawn there, and I often asked myself, 'Is the sun never going to rise high in this country?' I found it quite impossible to guess where it was in the sky from the condition of the light, which was not only unnaturally low, but also shot through and through with an all-pervasive grey.

After seeing this light I understood why an English Viceroy of India would never remain out of doors except in the early morning even in the cold season, and also why, when I was showing the sights of Delhi to a distinguished English man of letters on a cloudy and grey day, he said that he was better able to feel the grandeur and beauty of the Qutb Minar in that light than on the previous occasion when it was sunny, although that too was a day of our winter.

This light contributes to the sense of unreality. It also creates a mood of pensive wonder, so that a man from the tropics finds it impossible to be gay or blithe in England, although he may be very happy and even achingly joyous. If we were given to writing poetry we would have written Odes to Evening in the broad noon:

> *If aught of oaten stop or pastoral song*
> *May hope, O pensive Eve, to soothe thine ear*
> *Like thy own solemn springs,*
> *Thy springs, and dying gales....*

The Nymph Reserved was there at all times of the day.

But I wish to speak here, not so much of the psychological, as of the optical effect of this light. Everything in England presents itself to our eyes in a manner different from visual phenomena on the plains of India. We get a curious sense of the reality of the third dimension, which is perhaps most easily illustrated with reference to trees. Something I had noticed about them in England and France made me take a look at the extensive park which can be seen from the verandah of my flat in Delhi on the very morning I returned from abroad.

'There,' I said, 'those trees do look flat, and at midday when the hot winds will be blowing they will become a mirage.' The mango is of all the trees of the Indian plains the most plastic in appearance, but even it loses its roundness except during the rains when there is a good deal of moisture in the atmosphere. In the West the poplar furnishes an instance of the opposite kind. Among all the trees there it is the one which can be expected to look most like a paper cut-out. But even when leafless it keeps its plasticity. When I was in England the trees had not come into leaf, for they were all late that year with the exception of a few horse-chestnuts. Nevertheless the bare branches did not look fan-like as such branches do in India, they looked broom-like, and the rooks' nests emphasized the roundness. I was able to judge the real appearance of trees in the West in France.

But the effect is most powerfully and cleanly observed in architecture. I arrived in London one afternoon, and early next morning I was walking towards Hyde Park from a place near Albion Gate. It was, I believe, a normal residential locality, and in any case it had no features of any particular interest. But the whole scene affected me in a very queer way, and trying to account for this sensation of strangeness and even oddity, I found that to my eyes the houses were rising more steeply and perpendicularly from the pavement, forming a higher skyline, and altogether standing more four-square than anything in the way of houses I had seen doing in my own country, even in a big modern city like Calcutta.

The impression of solidity was so strong that if I had had a hammer in my hand I should have walked along unconsciously tapping the houses with it, and in a mood of impatience, which endless rows of brick and stone often generate, I should have involuntarily thought of a battering-ram, as in the same circumstances in India the idea of a volley of burning torches would have suggested itself to my mind.

When the architecture is fine the light sets off its proper beauty. In India I have never seen an architectural ensemble taking shape as does the Place Vendôme in Paris, or the courts and quads at Cambridge and Oxford, all of which seemed to convert even the enclosed air into cubes. I cannot remember any historic building in northern India, with the exception of the Taj at dawn, which conveys the feeling of mass. Our temples, big and soaring as they are, get lost in the upper air, and do not stand out as, for instance, I saw Winchester or Chartres doing. The beauty of our monuments is more like that of a clean-cut etching, it lies in their outline.

The three-dimensionality of the Western buildings is felt even in their interiors. In the spacious audience halls of the Muslim palaces and inside most of the mosques I have a sensation of extension in space confined only to a plane surface, before, behind, and to right and left. But in England and France the walls or pillars and the ceilings were always forcing themselves on my consciousness. My senses climbed up one set of piers, crawled across the ceiling, and came down again along the piers on the opposite side. I felt this most strongly in the Gothic cathedrals and the great chapels, like Henry VII's, St George's, King's College, but certainly it was equally perceptible in St Paul's as well as St Peter's.

Sir Edwin Lutyens, the English architect, became aware of this as soon as he arrived in India to plan and design the new capital in Delhi at the invitation of the Indian Government. He noticed that the fierce sun of the country disrupted architectural masses, and after examining the Mogul buildings he thought that their wide cornices or dripstones were meant to counteract the blurring effect of the light along the upper edges, by throwing a broad band of shadow and thus solidifying the top. Whether the Moguls had any such conscious motive or not, the optical effect observed by Lutyens is at all events real, as I have seen myself. This also explains why in India we not only tolerate but even yearn for a certain amount of corpulence in the human figure, both masculine and feminine. A bulk which in Regent's Park would be mistaken for that of a hippopotamus strayed from its enclosure, would, after the light of Delhi had played on it to produce its disruptive effect, only give to the physical presence of a man or woman its modicum of impressiveness.

Lutyens also spoke of the washing away of colour by the Indian sun, not of fading with time or being filmed with dust, but appearing far less deep than it really was at all times. In England I made the opposite discovery and found that colour in my country and colour there were quite different things. In our country we have many flowers with blazing colours, but these hues always seem to flow and run into the surrounding atmosphere, as dyes which are not fast do in water. In England and France on the other hand I saw floral colours almost as frozen masses, and for the first time understood the plastic function of colour in painting. All the flowers in the West had to my eyes a pronounced waxen appearance, and when they were the annuals I was familiar with in India—for we cultivate many English annuals in our country—they seemed to be quite different flowers. In borders and beds the English flowers looked like *pietra dura*, and in formal parterres, as in the Knot Garden of New Place at Stratford-upon-Avon, they seemed to have been woven into a vast Persian carpet.

Another striking effect of the light is seen in the English landscape, which seemed decidedly more stereoscopic to me than any visual reality I had been familiar with previously. I thought I was looking at everything through a pair of prismatic binoculars. In India any landscape tends to resolve into a silhouette, with a side-to-side linking of its components, in the West it becomes a composition in depth, with an into-the-picture movement, a recession, which carries the eye of the onlooker, wherever any opening is left, to the vanishing point on the horizon. The configuration of the country, the ever-present rolling aspect, accentuates the impression, as I found when I looked up a slope to a ring of trees or down a hill into a wooded hollow. I am not surprised to find Englishmen regarding flat country as dull, nor at their reading a figurative meaning into the phrase 'lie of the land', for being always aware of their position in space they quite spontaneously carry the association into the sphere of their actions and behaviour, matching geographical with psychological topography.

Moreover, whenever a landscape has been consciously laid out the natural appearance of the country not only inspires the design, it is even made more coherent and obvious. I felt this in every park of every great country house I saw, but most strongly perhaps when I was standing before the conservatory in Warwick Castle, inside which is the famous Warwick Vase. A peacock was walking on the terrace, steps led down to the formal garden, then the ground sloped towards the river to show a long stretch of gleaming water between wooded hills. It was a wholly traditional aspect of the English landscape, but to me it was novel to the point of being revolutionary.

The interiors of the houses were so disposed that they showed the aspects in the same way. While going through some of them, I could understand why Elizabeth Bennet ceased to look at the furniture at Pemberley, and went to a window, for I too found that outside objects were taking different positions from room to room; and that from every window there were beauties to be seen.

But perhaps even more than in landscape gardening the plastic vision finds a significant expression in the gardens themselves. Landscape after all is a collection of features disposed in space, but we think of a garden most naturally as a plane surface, with a two-dimensional pattern. But the English gardens become three-dimensional through variations of level. Until I had seen them with their terraces, sunk lawns, ponds and hedges, I could never imagine that gardens could be so architectural and even statuesque. I think I ought to stress the hedges, for they are linear by their very function, but in the Western gardens they had become cubic. Clipped yew, topiaries, or even formal gardens are unthinkable in the tropics. The formal gardens which the Moguls introduced in India are a wholly different kind of creation, a horticultural extension of the flat and linear Persian art.

All this must seem very trite. But what I want to do is to lead from these observed facts to a generalization which though not wholly new has been confirmed in me by experience. All art critics, and above all Roger Fry, have said that Oriental art is linear, whereas the Western is plastic, but they do not seem to have realized that this distinction was related to the natural appearance of the visual phenomena to the peoples of the two worlds. The different forms of art simply reflect the different appearances. An Indian who had seen only pictures by Constable but not the English landscape would not be very unreasonable if on seeing the landscape he argued that it was copied from the paintings. Yet there are clever people who think it fashionable to say that painting can be un-representational.

Is that why the contemporaneous preference in England was for Turner, to the neglect of Constable? The English ordinarily look at a picture for its story, characterization, romance, or, at a lower level, moral, and perhaps they found Constable's work too much like what they were always seeing, while Turner was putting in the light that never was on sea or land. Perhaps this too explains why the French, being more analytical, took to him immediately. I had come to regard Constable as the greatest English painter without in any way denying Turner's greatness. So it distressed me when I heard a painter friend of mine, whose judgement I respected, telling me after his return from England that to his thinking Turner was decidedly above Constable. But when I saw the original Constables myself and felt his passionate and revealing truthfulness, I wrote to say that I stuck to my old preference.

The third-dimensionality of the English scene seems to have influenced the visual evocations in English literature as well. There is a curious solidity and into-the-space movement in them too. From the top of Bredon Housman hears the bells ringing in all the shires from steeples far and near; Matthew Arnold sees the elm tree bright against the West, overlooking Ilsley Downs, the three lone weirs, and the youthful Thames; Wordsworth takes in at a glance ten thousand daffodils, stretched in never-ending line along the margin of the bay; even Milton pictures the fallen Satan in this way—

> *With head uplift above the wave, and eyes*
> *That sparkling blazed, his other parts besides*
> *Prone on the flood, extended long and large,*
> *Lay floating many a rood.*

If all this sounds very fanciful, there is at all events my experience of the English scene. After seeing it I have come to feel how idle it is to speak of an objective vision. We see the world as it dictates our way of seeing, we in the East in one, a *rarefied* way, and they in the West in another, a *concrete* way. I do not know *whether* these different ways of appearing also correspond to different ways of existing in reality. But to me even the differing vision was something like a shock. Alice, when she wanted to get rid of the fright which the Queen had given her by calling for her head, cried out, 'Who cares for *you*? You're nothing but a pack of cards!' I on the contrary exclaimed, 'Why, they are all cubes!' And I am not at all surprised that a super-logical set of Europeans should have invented a style of painting called Cubism.

III

OH, EAST IS EAST, AND WEST IS WEST...

As I READ KIPLING more and more I find that it is he who has said some of the truest, if also the bluntest, things about the relations of the East and the West, and I now think he need not have given utterance to that unconvincing afterthought of his. If indeed, as he wrote, there was neither East nor West when two strong men stood face to face, though they came from the ends of the earth, that exiguous bit of equality on a narrow strip of unadministered territory on the north-west frontier of British India can be ignored for all practical purposes. It may have given the Pathan the freedom to shoot a British soldier, and the British soldier a reciprocal freedom, but it has not made any difference to the irreconcilability of the two modes of human existence, one in the tropics and the other in temperate lands. The twain shall never meet.

Like all my countrymen who have read that dictum of Kipling's I rejected it violently. I was a believer in the accepted doctrine of the synthesis of the best in the East and the West, which of course meant substantial Westernization. Doubts, however, entered my mind as soon as I began to meet Occidentals in India, which I had not done except very casually until I had passed the age of fifty. By that time I had also seen the relapse of almost all my contemporaries into Hindu traditionalism of one kind or another. This gave me a warning of the superficiality of Westernization.

The visit to the West has converted my doubts into a certainty, and I have given up my old Westernizing shibboleths. I had not been there for even a week when I realized how impossible it was for either the East or the West to resemble each other in any significant trait. A few isolated individuals might by dint of a tremendous and costly effort and in very favourable circumstances bring about varying degrees of transformation, but for large human groups in either world to attempt to do so would be a suicidal revolt against Nature.

What divides the East from the West is neither Anglo-Saxon pride nor Hindu xenophobia. Both have indeed done their worst, but even they could not have made the division so unbridgeable without a contribution from something infinitely stronger, something which is absolutely basic to man's existence on earth—temperature. Speaking of life on the earth Robert Bridges wrote:

> *All its selfpropagating organisms exist*
> *only within a few degrees of the long scale*
> *rangeing from measured zero to unimagin'd heat,*
> *a little oasis of Life in Nature's desert;*
> *and ev'n therein our soft bodies vext and harm'd*
> *by their own small distemperature, nor could they endure*
> *wer't not that by a secret miracle of chemistry*
> *they hold internal poise upon a razor-edge*
> *that may not ev'n be blunted, lest we sicken and die.*

I could feel the working of this chemistry within me as long as I remained in the West.

There was indeed a time when people overrated rather than underrated the influence of temperature on human life. But man's success in refrigeration, which enables him to eat Australian beef and West Indian bananas in England has made him sadly arrogant. I see this illustrated almost every day in India. The old British official in his sola topee could not escape the heat, and by bringing about a psychological adaptation it endowed him with a sense of the possible which was almost the same as wisdom. But in the artificial cool of the air-conditioned room the Indian and his Occidental friends alike acquire the habit of reckoning without the host. They overlook the relentless control of temperature on human endeavour.

Thus with them the horizon bounding the possible recedes farther and farther until the word 'impossible' is sincerely believed to exist only in the dictionary of fools. For the Indian minister or official the mere discussion of his plans with an Occidental in an air-conditioned room is equivalent to execution. The Occidental too shares the vision and shows an inexhaustible facility in smiling, assenting and paying compliments, which would have been surprising if one did not remember that while in India he too was as carefully protected against the dissolving influence of heat as the New Zealand butter sold in the country. In India the mirages of the mind are produced by coolness.

But if a man allows the natural differences of temperature to have their proper effect on him and argues on the basis of that experience it will not be long before he will arrive at a more realistic estimate of the differing potentialities of man, beast, and plant in different climates. I have described the immediate effect which my transit from one climate to another produced on me, but I got an inkling of a much bigger truth even before I had actually landed in England.

After leaving Delhi I was flying for a whole day over the deserts of Rajputana, the rocky Baluchistan coast, the promontory of Oman, to land just before evening at Bahrein. I was terror-stricken by the colour and configuration of the country below me, tawny, red or grey; wavy, jagged, or dead flat. As we were flying over Oman, I kept my eyes fixed in a fascinated stare on the country below, and the English accountant remarked, 'Like the moon, isn't it?' Bahrein was not so frightening, but it was not a whit less stark. The sea was quite close to the runway, and almost at the same level with the wide stretch of grey sand. The only thing which enabled me to distinguish between the two was the roll of the sea.

Another aircraft left for Karachi before us, and as its passengers were going on board I heard the crowing of a baby, and saw an English child being carried in its cradle basket. I could not help asking myself, 'What the devil is it going to do in that galley?' The aeroplane took off and flew away in a south-easterly direction. Although it was going to the only country of which I had any direct perception, the country which was the home and shelter of my body and spirit, I found it hard to believe that the aeroplane was not spiriting away the child to

Ultima Thule. The departing aeroplanes produced quite a different effect the next morning at Frankfurt. They seemed in no way more unusual than departing trains at a railway station.

One night divided the East from the West on that journey, and when I woke up the next morning to see a beautifully tilled and green country below me I thought it was the famous Campania, the country round Naples. I asked the stewardess, 'How long will it be before we reach Rome?' 'We are coming down on it,' she replied. So it was really Campagna Romana. Presently we landed on Ciampino.

I saw equally smiling country as I flew over northern Italy, Germany, Belgium and Kent. Curiously enough neither the large stretches of the Apennines, which I saw partly in their barren russet tint and partly covered with fleecy snow, nor even the sharp and bluish-white Alpine peaks which rose through the clouds as if to cut the aeroplane to shreds, could give me any sensation of fear.

It came to me in a flash. I realized that I was seeing a new mode of human existence on the face of the earth, and I said to myself: 'In the East man is either a parasite on Nature or her victim, here man and Nature have got together to create something in common.'

Such precipitate theorizing is worse than meeting trouble half-way, some people will say. But I think I can retort that many of the most far-reaching scientific theories were arrived at, not by laborious induction or by working out statistical averages, but all of a sudden in a spark of intuition. In any case there is the saying, Clerk Maxwell's if I am not mistaken, that you have only to put forward a hypothesis for the proofs to follow. I found them coming along soon enough.

Since almost everything that I am going to say will be, in one way or another, a setting down of these proofs, I think all that I have to do here is to amplify the statement I have just made, so that there may be no room for doubt as to what I have in mind, whether it be true or not.

The first stretch of the English countryside that I saw was Kent, or as much of it as I could see when going to Canterbury from London by way of Maidstone and returning through Rochester. A few days later I saw more, a good deal of Berkshire and Wiltshire, on my way to Bristol. What struck me immediately was the amount of green. It was not the green of the trees, which were leafless. The Burnham beeches, when I saw them, were bare, and it was after going to France that I understood the meaning of the phrase 'beechen green', which I had read as a boy. In England it was the green of the grass. It was set off very charmingly by the black and white or brown and white of the cattle, and creamy white of the sheep and lambs, which lay like bundles of fleece on the meadows. I had no conception that industrial and over-populated England could look so thoroughly pastoral.

I knew, of course, that there was a logical connection between the green of the grass and the over-population, but this again is English or rather Western logic. In my country over-population leads to greater and ever greater embrownment, to a deadly feud between tillage on the one hand and pasture and woods on the other.

As I looked at these hundreds of square miles of typical English scenery, I said to myself that there was man's hand in it everywhere. It was too much like landscape gardening on a vast and countrywide scale to be anything but man's work in its final appearance. In fact, one could perhaps say that the landscape gardening of the late eighteenth century was only the last and conscious phase of an unconscious landscape gardening which had been going on in England for ages, a process which had removed even from the wildest English scene all traces of wildness as understood in the tropical East.

But it was not also man's work in our sense of it. For wherever in the East the hungry generations of men have marched on Nature they have come like ruthless colonists, who have sacked the countries they have conquered. It is not for nothing that the villages of the Gangetic plain look like field fortifications, a collection of trenches and earthworks, and that men stand at bay in the fields, among a corn which is always alien to its surroundings. For these men Nature, so far as it has been subjugated, is like their cattle—starved, twisted in the tail, and goaded; and so far as it is wild is like the wild beasts—for then it means flood, dust storm, cyclone, creeping weed or sand, and locusts. They live at the mercy of Nature, get very little from it, and take their revenge by making ceaseless war on it.

So far from seeing man in this role in the English countryside, I hardly saw him at all. It all seemed strangely silent and solitary to me. In France I saw more evidence of man's presence, even if I did not see as much as I do in India. I saw peasants bending over the crops as they are shown doing in the paintings of Millet. In England I saw the work of the peasant and the herdsman everywhere, but not them.

Thus the more I saw the more was I reminded of my initial generalization, the elimination of the dividing line between man's work and Nature's. I was seeing a world where nothing was quite natural, and nothing quite artificial either, in which, actually, both the adjectives were more or less out of place. It was an existence in which I did not find that spectacle so familiar to me—man's cruel and endless struggle with Nature.

When I put forward this idea tentatively in one of my articles a fellow-Bengali commented somewhat sneeringly that it was a Wordsworthian conception of the relationship between Nature and Man. How true he was, and really how complimentary! I can now understand why those who wanted us Indians to imbibe the spirit of English life through literature made us read so much of Wordsworth. But I also see why this reading failed substantially to achieve its purpose.

IV

BY THE RIVERS OF ENGLAND

THERE I SAT DOWN, and if actually I did not weep, I felt very deeply moved. This was unexpected in a Bengali, because he is disposed to be rather scornful of the English rivers, looking upon them as no better than canals. This, however, is most often a dutiful patriotic gesture, prompted by the fear of seeming to be disloyal to the gorgeous waters of Bengal. Those Bengalis with whom the feeling for their rivers is not mere nationalistic sentiment but genuine love and an influence on sensibility are bound to be touched as I was, by the peculiar aspect of water in England.

I should explain, however, that I shall have nothing to say about what many would regard as the most important aspect, and quite rightly. I mean the sea-front of the country, the seafaring life of the people, and the impact of the sea on their spirit. I have indeed always been conscious of all this. As I have written in my autobiography, even as a boy I had learnt to consider the sea as an appanage and projection of England. 'Combined visions of land and sea were always fleeting through my mind and before my eyes whenever I tried to think of England. Of only one other country in the world did I ever think in that way when I was a boy, and that was ancient Greece.' But the blue water will be absent from this account because I did not see it. I did not go to England by sea, and curiously enough I never went to any coastal town, not even Brighton.

So I missed the grandest aspect of the English people's relations with water. But to my thinking the inland waters of the country are not any the less interesting. Having been born and brought up in early life in East Bengal, a country of rivers, I found in the rivers of England not only a scenic complement and contrast to what I was familiar with, but also complements and contrasts of mood and emotion. To make this intelligible I shall begin by giving an idea of my own experience of inland waters, both in Bengal and elsewhere, for it was this which made me see the English rivers in the way I did.

We Bengalis have no difficulty in understanding why a god of water was called Proteus, because if anything has a bewildering variety of forms in Bengal it is the waters. I last saw them more than thirty years ago, but they are still before me in recollection: the great rivers warm-toned and foamy, heaving and swift, and in their eddies, swirls, and dancing waves seeming to run like endless shoals of dolphins before the steamers; the lazy small streams winding in such a manner through the jungle that all one could see from a boat was a ribbon of water of about the length of a coot's dive disappearing round the corner, which made our boatmen reply, 'So many windings', whenever we asked them how much farther we had still to go; the more open 'broads', in places shining, in places sown with lilies, with deep green weed showing through the water, and reeds at the edges; and even our man-made tanks, artificial in their rectangularity, but in no way more so than anything in Nature marked out by man, say a field.

It is hardly likely that I shall set eyes on them again. The rivers I have been seeing since then are those of the Gangetic plain, wild and sacred at the same time. During the monsoons they become broad and rushing channels of flood, often very destructive, and in the cold season, under a blue-grey sky, they look like a chain of lagoons in a desolate landscape of sandbanks. On these water-fowl settle in their thousands— ducks, storks, cranes, ibises, flamingoes, spoonbills, avocets, stints, snipe, and many other species. At the approach of man they rise in wild alarm with screams and whirr of wings.

These rivers have no truck with man. They flow past the biggest cities in northern India without so much as a nod of recognition on either side. For example, topographically, nothing is more external to Delhi than the Jumna, a river more romanticized in Indian literature than any other. But we have ceased long since to place our idylls or for that matter even our assignations by the rivers. Today, standing on the bank of the

Jumna, a man would hardly suspect that the capital of India was just behind him.

The secular government of India becomes aware of the rivers when they threaten the cities with flood, or dry up to endanger the water supply. Then it sends out its sappers and miners to the rescue. The people of India, more religious than their government, remain in touch with the rivers through Hinduism. The cult of the rivers is much older in our country than many other cults supposed to be very ancient. The big rivers are sacred all over the country, and they were sacred even before the great gods migrated to their banks. As a matter of fact, they migrated to take advantage of a pre-existing holiness. All Hindus flock to these rivers to bathe and purify themselves, to jettison some of the accumulation of worldliness. In Delhi I see streams of people going to have their daily dip in the Jumna every morning, and on days of the new moon or festivals colourful processions of village women march to and from the river. For this reason, if any cities in India have a river front, it is only the cities sacred to Hinduism—Hardwar, Mathura, and Benares. But we Hindus have never tried to bring human life and the rivers together.

In England and France I seemed to have forgotten the immediate past in a fit of amnesia, and gone back to the waters of my childhood. Ermenonville, with its woods, *étangs*, and blackbirds' song reminded me of my mother's village, although that village was only the wild and primitive ancestress of the sophisticated French park. I had similar feelings even in Paris. Standing on one or other of the Seine bridges at dusk I recovered, across the decades that had come in between, the peace I used to feel only by the rivers of East Bengal.

This had happened in England too, before I had gone to France. But there was a very important difference between my feelings about the rivers of my boyhood and those of England. In East Bengal, whenever we went near water or water came near us, we became aquatic in spirit. I could well imagine myself to be a carp or an eel, but in England I was astonished to discover how near to land water could approach. Everywhere it was closely interwoven with the life and landscape on *terra firma*.

This becomes more interesting if one remembers the duality of the geographical appearance of England, the contrast between the country's seaward face and inland face, which makes for a double personality. For an island with a very striking pelagic aspect, the interior is curiously land-bound. No point inside the country is more than seventy-five miles or so from tidal water, yet it is not possible to find any sign of the nearness of the sea once it is out of sight. There is no belt of transition, mangrove swamps, coconut palm groves, sand dunes, or even estuarial waters as we see in India. Wordsworth heard the soft inland murmur of the Wye not very far from the coast, and at Bristol, even with the small ships in the docks near Queen Square, I had difficulty in believing that the sea was only about ten miles away.

The people on their part lose their pelagic outlook no less thoroughly. These seafarers behave inland as if they had never heard of the sea, and adapt themselves to the earth in a manner I should not have thought natural in any but burrowing animals. That is why they can write an allegory of national life with rats, toads, moles and badgers as heroes. What surprised me was not solely this, but the assimilation of water to this kind of life, and to the earthy aspect of the landscape. I had a vague presage of this from English literature, but I never expected to see such land-clinging waters actually with my own eyes.

Of course, I knew that even in England water could be destructive. I had read of floods, and of the devastation at Lynmouth in Devon in 1952. But what I have just pointed out may perhaps be regarded as the normal aspect of water in the country, in which it is not only a part of the English terrestrial landscape, but also an element in English life and civilization.

If I may say so, the waters of England are like their own swans, wild in origin but cultivated in behaviour. No one who wants to get into the spirit of the English rivers should ignore these noble, strong, and, if occasion demands, fighting birds. I saw them almost wherever there was water, even in a gravel pit which had become a lake. But the most vivid recollection I have of them is from Stratford-upon-Avon. They were always swimming in the river. One morning, however, they gave a more stirring display.

I had gone out to take my usual morning walk, always taken between half past five and seven, when I found the English scene to be both at its most serene and at its most communicative. The

English people with their confirmed late-rising habit, which I thought was most considerate of them, then left their country to me, almost wholly I might say. I found the swans going about in batches of three or four as usual, but all of a sudden for no reason that I could see a very magnificent cob worked itself up to a fit of temper, and puffing up its wings bore down on the others like a great galleon. He charged and busked again and again until all the other birds were driven through the arches beyond the bridge.

The Avon at Stratford is a tranquil river, but one day walking along its bank a little farther than my usual round I perceived a certain animation in the water, and shortly afterwards a rush. 'What can be the matter?' I asked myself, and as I looked downstream in the direction of the current, I saw large flakes of foam skimming away on the surface of the water. Then I read the notice about the weir. The same Avon at Warwick looked rather like a hill stream, although even there it was linked to the overhanging Castle, or the Castle was to the river, the result being the same.

But perhaps I got the strongest impression of what I would call the 'terrestriality' of water when going to Cambridge and at Cambridge itself. From the train, which was passing through a typical countryside of tillage and pasture, I saw what looked like sails of yachts gliding along, apparently on dry ground. As I am used to seeing sails only between the blue of the sky and the grey-green of rivers, these seemed almost ghostly to me. But presently a narrow strip of water came in view, and I asked what that river was. It was the Lea, I was told.

The next morning I was sitting in the lounge of the hotel gazing beyond the garden at the meadows, which I believe are called Sheep's Green, wholly overlooking the river between the two. Some very fine Friesians were cropping grass in a leisurely manner, and their strong markings were somewhat softened by a very fine drizzle. All of a sudden a majestic swan floated past making me aware of the Cam, or is it Granta? Even there I could see a slight motion in the water and hear a very slight murmur, for a weir was near by. I wished the old mill still stood, so that I could see one, for to my thinking nothing brings the idea of water and earth together so closely as a mill, which employs

water to make bread, the gift of Mother Earth who bears the
name of Ceres or Demeter.

Even in the outskirts of London one feels this interweaving
of land and water. In London proper the Thames has certainly
become different from what it was in Tudor times and down
to the middle of the eighteenth century when Canaletto painted
it; but going to Hampton Court by steamer I could see that the
spirit of the old times was still on the river. From Kew onwards
it took on a very sylvan appearance in the English sense, that
is to say, without wildness and at the same time without an
industrial or even urban atmosphere. All along its banks parks
alternated with houses, and the sudden vision of Syon House
with its lion reminded one of the presence of a very sophisticated civilization on the edge of the water. Hampton Court Park
and Palace followed naturally, and it was not difficult to imagine
that the Palace was still a royal residence.

On the river I found a scene which was equally characteristic. It was a Saturday afternoon, and a strong breeze was
blowing. The river was full of boats and yachts, and it seemed
to me as if some sort of regatta was going on. I had never before
seen so many sails packed so closely together in so narrow a
stretch of water. At times a yacht would come heading straight
for the steamer, and only a frantic tussle and scuffle with the
tiller and ropes would narrowly avert a collision.

Yet a very large number of ducks were swimming on the
river between the boats, and off and on more would come and
alight on it. As I had never seen wild ducks behaving in that way
I asked if the birds were domesticated. 'All completely wild,' I
was told. Then I asked whether nobody shot them. This time
the answer was only a smile.

V

WHO MADE THE TOWN?

AFTER COMING BACK FROM England, I have often wondered why even before the Industrial Revolution the English language came to have the saying: 'God made the country, and man made the town.' Cowper, who seems to have given the epigram, though not perhaps the idea, to his countrymen, not only placed health and virtue in the country and accused the town of scaring away the thrush and offending the nightingale, he laid a much greater iniquity at its door. The town's mirth, he thought, was public mischief and a plague to the realm, because in his view the townsmen had done what even the worst enemies of England had failed to do, namely, make the British Empire a mutilated structure, soon to fall, whose archstone would have remained steadfast but for the town fops who should have wielded fans instead of wearing swords. Obviously, he had only London in mind. But as he phrased it, the indictment was sweeping and general.

With English education we in India, too, took over the stock theme, and at school I myself wrote a number of essays on it, loading the scales heavily against the town. But as soon as I actually saw the English towns I came to see the artificial didacticism of the anti-town pose. Neither the thrush nor the blackbird had been driven out of London, for I was awakened by their song in the heart of the town. What I have to say further about London will be set down later. Here I shall deal only with the smaller English towns.

To me it seemed that these towns had as much right to belong to the country as any village in England. The two appeared to be of a piece with each other, indeed so much so that I should not have been able to tell a village street from a town street but for its less busy air and fewer shops. At the most the difference was one of size and population, that is to say, a matter of degree and not kind, and thus inessential and unimportant.

If I had to single out any one thing as a discovery in the way of human habitation in my experience I would say it was the English country towns. In India the country towns are very much worse than the big cities. They have all the squalor of their overgrown relatives but none of the amenities. In England, on the contrary, the smaller towns seemed to be wholly different from the cities, and a species by themselves. Some of them might be market towns, some cathedral towns, some manufacturing towns, and yet others university towns. Nonetheless, all of them had a family likeness which was not effaced by their differing functions, just as the family likeness of brothers is not by their different professions.

What is more important is that the towns fit perfectly into their surroundings and at the same time give a point of dramatic human interest to the countryside, enliven it. If I may put it this way, they convert what would otherwise have been still life, *nature morte*, into a living genre picture. I suppose too that economically they are as closely interwoven with the countryside as they are in appearance.

These towns appeared to be very complex inside, a maze of streets and lanes, and it was the easiest thing to lose one's way in them. One even lost sight of the cathedral, big as it was. Although I saw the towers of Canterbury Cathedral as a landmark from the country, when I was in the town I could not guess where it was even from the High Street or for that matter from Mercery Lane. The same thing happened to me at Chartres, and in London as well. After following St Paul's all the way from Westminster Bridge and along the Embankment, I lost sight of it near Black-friars Bridge, and had the humiliation of having to ask a policeman where it was. At Winchester the Cathedral called me to itself with its bells, but I could not see it once I was in the town. It was a Sunday morning, and as I got down from the train it began to rain. I was without umbrella or overcoat, and began to run to the right or to the left, always following the beautiful peal, which is so much like stained glass in sound, until I found shelter within the Cathedral.

But in these towns it is not long before one finds oneself in the open country, from where you see a steeple, tower, dome, or keep, which not only gives you back your bearings, but also makes you feel how one or other of these holds the town together. The countryside also converges on it along the roads:

> Sometimes a troop of damsels glad,
> An abbot on an ambling pad,
> Sometimes a curly shepherd-lad,
> Or long-haired page in crimson clad,
> Goes by to towered Camelot.

It is not necessary to go to Mont St Michel to find that a manmade structure can be the focus of a still landscape of fields and waters. I saw this at Ely, Cambridge, St Albans, Winchester, Warwick, and indeed in every English town I went to. No contrast was more intriguing than that which existed between the extreme simplicity of their *raison d'etre* and the complexity of their internal organization.

Indeed, if I had a mind to be clever I would have completely reversed the antithesis between the town and the country in England. I would have said that there it was man who had made the country and God the town, pointing to the park and the cathedral in justification.

But there is no doubt either that in former ages Englishmen did get a stronger impression of the contrast between their towns and their villages than I did or contemporary Englishmen do. Just as today, living in an industrial and state-run society, we tend to jumble up the land-owning gentleman, squire, merchant of the old type, artisan, and peasant in one social genus against the new genus formed by the industrialist, bureaucrat, financier, technician, and workman, in the same way we also mix up the whole of the English landscape as it had developed down to the Industrial Revolution in one picture to be set against all that has made its appearance since. The coming of the modern megalopolis has certainly made us less capable of noticing the distinction between the country and the old English towns. To the people of the pre-industrial era it must have been very real, for it divided parliamentary representation between the boroughs and the shires, created two forms of local government, and made all sorts of other differences. What was that due to?

An immediate and partial explanation is that the consciously formulated and didactic antithesis was a literary convention, reflecting an acquired moral attitude, both being the result of a classical education. The writers and with them their readers enjoyed being sententious and rhetorical in the vein of the Latin poets. In England, it would seem, the poets were on the side of the country and the men of letters on that of the town; if Cowper was the most shrinking of the countrymen, Dr Johnson was the most robust of the town-dwellers.

But where had the Latin poets themselves got that from? They were the children of a city, the most colossal city-state ever seen in the world, and many of them were quite proud of the empire their city had grown into. Therefore, I think, in order to explain their paradoxical moral attitude, one has to go far back into the past of the peoples conventionally called Aryans. They were a folk of forests and grassland who had no love or even friendliness for cities. An old inscription from Ur speaks of a host whose onslaught was like a hurricane, and who had never known a city. Even after they had come into the Mediterranean world to adopt and get used to city life they never quite conquered the antipathy which lingered in their mind.

In ancient India, too, the Aryans seem to have felt the same aversion. Brahmanism is not kind to cities. In Kalidasa's famous play, *Shakuntala*, two ascetics are made to give expression to the dislike when they come to a city. One says that he is feeling as if he was in a house which was on fire, and the other replies that he is looking on the pleasure-loving townsfolk as a man who has bathed does on those who are still smeared with oil. At the beginning of the nationalist movement we Hindus used to throw it in the teeth of the Europeans that their civilization was one of cities whereas ours was the product of the sacred woods, implying of course that ours was very much superior.

The English people had certainly inherited this dislike at one remove. These children of the northern forests remembered the original strangeness of the things from the Mediterranean world, which afterwards became an essential element in the new civilization of their own creation. Thus they felt as foreign, not only the towns, but other things as well, for instance, Latinity in their language and classicism in their architecture. This emotional resistance still lurks.

But what they were and sometimes are prone to overlook is their extraordinary success in handling the elements from the Mediterranean world, of which the English language provides the most striking illustration. When I saw the English towns of the pre-industrial age I recognized another hardly less striking success. I felt as if these towns which they had taken over from the south and anglicized thoroughly were only complements to the English rural landscape. I was standing one morning in the market square of Devizes, where a brisk canvassing of all kinds of merchandise was going on. From a motor van a man, recognized as a Londoner from his accent by my companion, was hawking dress fabrics. He was combining the old and the new salesmanship very effectively, and was perfectly in place in that charming old-world market, to which the girl who sang 'The Next Market Day' must have been going.

I was keenly interested in the people and the scene, and suddenly I saw a cross with an inscription on it. Going up to it I read the story of a woman, Ruth Pierce by name if I am not mistaken, who had tried to cheat her companions and had fallen dead as soon as she had said that she should be struck dead by God if she was lying. The inscription began with the words:

> The Mayor and Corporation of Devizes avail themselves of the stability of this building to transmit to future times the record of an awful event which occurred in this market place in the year 1753, hoping much that such record may serve as a salutary warning against the danger of impiously invoking the Divine Vengeance in calling on the Holy name of God to conceal the devices of falsehood and fraud.

I could not think of anything more English.

But what of Bath, the nearby town? That is a legitimate question. I had read about Bath, but until I saw it, I had no idea how thoroughly Mediterranean it was. Not even Rome or Paris was more consistently Latin than this northern town. Standing in Lansdown Crescent, and looking towards Prior Park, if only the light were golden, I could imagine that I was looking towards the Alban Hills from the Capitol. In the Circus I felt the Latin spirit even more strongly, more than in the Piazza dell' Esedra. Then, there was the Guildhall. I was charmed with its Banqueting Room, the rows of Chippendale chairs, and the grand chandeliers, which they lighted for me. Guildhall is a northern word with northern visual suggestions. One expects to meet there burghers with pronounced Germanic looks, if not the Pied Piper himself. But they were inconceivable in that room. A strict John Bull might even have said that it was fit only for the dandies who had the manners of a dancing master and the morals of a whore. Besides, it is only at Bath that the inscription in Greek—'Ariston Men Hudor'—on the architrave below the pediment of the Pump Room sounds perfectly natural. Even at Oxford a similar inscription would have been slightly self-conscious. Thus it seemed to me that the only thing which was alien to Bath was the Abbey. The Gothic style, which looks congruous even in nineteenth-century London, strikes a discordant note at Bath.

But its classicism is neither imposed nor exotic. It is not a Brighton Pavilion on a large scale. England never got any of her Mediterranean features through Roman rule or any kind of imposition. In fact, imposed things, even when they survive, remain wholly foreign there and suggest only lifelessness. In spite of Kipling, I must say that it is quite impossible to raise the ghost of a centurion even on the Roman Wall, although one might catch a glimpse of Puck, Sir Richard, or St George himself. When I saw the Roman theatre at St Albans in the midst of English fields I felt its utter forlornness, it was a ruin without atmosphere. Although I brought back a shard of the second century which was given to me by one of the keepers, I cannot conjure up old Verulamium from it as I can the Roman Forum from the piece of marble I picked up from the foot of the partly restored little Temple of Vesta which stands opposite the Temple of Antoninus and Faustina. Everything given to Britain directly by Rome is dead, and everything borrowed mechanically remains stillborn. I wonder what a monstrosity a Roman aqueduct would have looked in England had any been built.

Bath gives material expression to the inward classicism of the English people, who have two souls, one northern and the other southern. Bath was created in an age when one of these souls was dominant, in the most Augustan and classical age in the existence of the English people as even the epoch of their Renaissance was not. It was an age in which an English statesman, recalling his life on his deathbed, could recite Homer, when Englishmen possessed a Latinity which could be condescending even to Italy and Rome. Georgina, Duchess of Devonshire, wrote from Italy that there was nothing in England which gave a better idea of the buildings and villas of Italy than dear Chiswick, and there was nothing in Italy in better taste. They thought they had out-Palladioed Palladio and out-Horaced Horace. Incidentally, the idea of the classicism of Bath which I had got from books was of this sort, the purest form of English classicism.

Therefore, when thinking of the Mediterranean elements in the landscape, life, and civilization of England, it is half the story to speak only of transformation, but it is wholly misleading to speak of borrowing, or of the intrusion of Latinity. A man might as well say that he was born of one parent with mere borrowings from the other. What has really happened is fusion, and in this process of fusion fixed formulas will never be discovered. The process has had an immense range of gradations, and it has always maintained a slow oscillation between two poles, one Anglo-Saxon, romantic, and septentrional, and the other Latin, classical, and meridional, and each of its products of every kind—personality, building, literary style—has justified itself, or for that matter failed to do so.

Even before going to England I had come to feel like that. Indeed I have never had any rigid criterion of anglicism, although I have a natural leaning towards a rather strict sort of purism in many things. I never thought that Sir Thomas Browne, or Milton, or Gibbon was less English than any other writer supposedly more so. I never quarrelled with the hotchpotch of Shakespeare's geography and ethnology. So when I saw the country, I was not bothered overmuch by the question of congruity and incongruity in styles.

Of course, the question would arise in my mind because I was aware of the existence of a controversy. For instance, standing on King's Parade at Cambridge I did consider if the white classical buildings by Gibbs clashed with King's College Chapel. I also wondered whether there was any conflict between Market Hill and the stately side of the street opposite, the academic facade of Cambridge. Again, strolling through the Backs or passing to them through the courts, I reviewed the moot question of the appropriateness of the architectural ensemble opposite, the much disputed University Library and Clare New Building. But I was also able to dismiss these questions. In England I did not mind ten times the incongruity that I would have resented in Paris or Rome. In fact, I have not seen one building which is as incongruous in England as is the Victor Emmanuel Monument in Rome by the side of the Capitol and in front of the Palazzo Venezia. The mingling of styles seemed to be quite natural in England. So I liked Bath as much as I liked Canterbury, and I thought that both were equally English.

VI

The Palazzo And The Basilica

Italianate as England has been in many things from time to time, I am not going to consider that subject at all. All that I have in mind is the metamorphosis of two other things which the English people have brought over from the Mediterranean and made completely their own. These are the Roman basilica transformed into the Gothic cathedral by the northern faith of the Middle Ages, and the Italian palazzo converted into the country house by the humanity of the Renaissance.

It has now become impossible to think of the English landscape without the one or the other. Both are its highlighted features, just as the village and the town are its larger toned-down details. The country houses are a rather more complex adaptation than the cathedrals, and I shall say something of my sensation of these first.

The first country house I saw was Knole (*clarum et venerabile nomen!*), which many will say was the best of beginnings. I had no difficulty in placing it or any other country house in the physical geography of England. They were like the diamond or sapphire in a beautiful piece of jewellery or an aria in an opera. Yet not quite. They did not push back their surroundings as the stone did the setting or the solo voice the orchestra. With them both the central piece and the setting were almost equally important, as the parts are in chamber music. Some even preferred the adjuncts to the main thing. As Elizabeth Bennet's aunt said, 'If it were a fine house richly furnished I should not care about it myself; but the grounds are delightful. They have some of the finest woods in the country.'

That, however, was going too far towards the other extreme. Of course, the timber was an essential part of these houses. Their builders and occupiers were northern lords who belonged to the land like the peasant and to the forest like the primitive hunter, and therefore they also wanted to take their homes as far towards the woods as possible. But they also wanted to live in a palace and in the country at the same time. Thus their houses came to illustrate most effectively the unity of architecture and landscape.

I admired the thoroughness in working out the interrelation. In the first place, the house could always be seen as the main feature of the composition. Even when a traveller passed quickly by its grounds he could recognize its presence through the number of vistas that led the eye to it. As I was coming to Oxford by train from Leamington I saw an organization of landscape like this. 'Is that a country house?' I asked. 'Rousham House', was the reply. On the other hand, it was equally impossible to overlook the surroundings from the interiors of the houses, however beautifully furnished and self-sufficient in aesthetic appeal they might be.

I could also see the subtlety of the transition. The houses were made to merge gradually into the landscape. First, there was the building, then the terrace, after that the formal garden, then the English garden, next the park, and last of all the wide countryside. A sightseer passed from the one to the other without becoming conscious of the transition, although it must have been consciously thought out.

I know that many consider the house itself to be the least harmonious part of some of these splendid compositions. I had read enough about the subject to have acquired some preconceptions in this respect. So, when I saw Blenheim Palace I endorsed, and quite sincerely, the orthodox view that it was somewhat alien to its beautiful surroundings. Perhaps if I had seen Chatsworth I should have felt in the same way, although that place had been legendary to me since my young days on account of what it contained.

But I do not think anyone can quite decidedly put his finger on what does or does not constitute the pure anglicism of a country house. Is it brick and wood as opposed to stone, a straggling facade as against a symmetrical one, irregular instead of a serried fenestration, gables against pediment, a sloping roof instead of a flat one, battlements against balustrade, being built, added to and altered through the centuries instead of being built once and for all, and so on and so forth? Each of these seems to matter and yet not matter, and in the end one is left with a subjective reaction, which nevertheless gives a very acutely felt notion that the line of the permissible has been passed.

In my case, I thought I had discovered a principle. I took a dislike to a house if it suggested in any way the modern palace of an Indian Maharaja. But this was no test at all, because these modern Indian palaces were themselves copied from the more grandiose or magniloquent English houses. That made my supposed principle only an aesthetic back-formation without independent value. At last, left without a criterion, I have decided, if ever I get another chance of seeing the country houses, to allow myself a good deal of latitude, and have only preferences but no exclusions.

So much for the physical geography of the country houses. I had, however, the greatest difficulty in relating them to the human geography of the country. As I contemplated them from the outside they appeared to stand aloof from every kind of human life, and not simply contemporary life in England. These strangely silent and quiet places looked like the palaces on hills and on the edge of woods about which one reads in fairy tales. The very first sight of Knole produced such an impression of unworldliness in me that as I pushed open the front door, the Outer Wicket I believe they call it, I half expected to meet Puss-in-Boots in the passage, and I cannot say that I found it quite natural or that I was relieved to come only upon the ladies who show the visitors round.

Before I saw them I thought I should see some animation around them. I did not indeed expect the pageantry of the Tudor times, nor even an illustration of the one-time relations between the English landowner and his tenant, as seen by Ben Jonson:

> There's none, that dwell about them, wish them downe;
> But all come in, the farmer, and the clowne:

> *And no one empty-handed to salute*
> *Thy lord, and lady, though they have no sute.*
> *Some bring a capon, some a rurall cake,*
> *Some nuts, some apples; some that thinke they make*
> *The better cheeses, bring' hem: or else send*
> *By their ripe daughters, whom they would commend*
> *This way to husbands; and whose baskets beare*
> *An embleme of themselves, in plum or peare.*

All that was of the past. But at all events I expected to see something of the owners and their families, or for that matter of their servants, some coming and going, or walking about and playing in the grounds. I expected some indication of the kind of life lived in these houses in the late nineteenth and early twentieth centuries, about which I had read in the biographies and memoirs, but I saw nothing of these things or of the inmates.

Once I caught a glimpse of the aged owner of one of these houses, dressed in the plainest possible clothes imaginable on the back of a peer—or am I wrong, those clothes being the only natural ones for such backs? At another place the guide suddenly exclaimed that the Marchioness was getting down from her car. On another occasion a duchess was casually referred to as the accessory of the magnificent writing desk we were looking at, and at which she worked every evening. It was only after going through the interiors of some of these houses that I was able to form some conception from the atmosphere and material signs of the role they played as contemporary human habitations. I shall, however, speak about this later, because, whether considered as lifeless heirlooms or living homes, these interiors belong to the cultural life of contemporary England.

The cathedrals on their part set me a far less difficult problem. They are less affected by changing sensibilities and fashions, and although they are the creations of a particular kind of sensibility, they still possess the power, so far as they possess any power at all, to deal with mankind on their own terms. Their function and purpose are as clear today as when they were built. Their presence was simpler than that of the country houses, though at the same time it was much more elemental, august, and transcendent. I have seen some great temples and mosques in my own country, and have felt how they ennobled a landscape. But the Gothic cathedrals seemed to me to possess this power to ennoble even more intensely and consistently. These structures were like lighthouses on land, sending out their beams day and night. Nevertheless, they appeared to have grown out of the soil as much as the country houses. I could not imagine that edifices which were so over-powering as architecture—and were bound to be, because in nothing else has architecture been nearer to perfection than in the buildings designed for the service of religion—could mingle so happily with a landscape of woods and fields.

But perhaps this was one of the things they were expressly meant to do. I have a notion that the northern Christians built the cathedrals to offset their native and primaeval forests, which were either heathen or pagan in feeling. I have heard that some of them were built on the sites of Druidical groves. These forests, which belonged to the Celto-German heritage of the European peoples, opposed their animism to the idea of the Christian God. I felt this when I saw the forests of Chantilly and Fontainebleau. At one stage of their existence they were only game preserves. But they also have a prehistory. Walking through them one expects to meet not only the lord, the hunter and the hound, but also a long procession extending far back into time of faun and nymph, and, still farther back, of fairy, gnome, dwarf and leprechaun.

When the Graeco-Roman heritage came into their life from the Mediterranean lands these northerners were faced with the problem of reconciling the two elements. In India, placed in an analogous situation, the Brahmanic civilization made an outcaste of the town. The Europeans behaved quite differently. They neither cut down the forests to replace them with brick and stone, nor did they reject urban civilization. They tried to bring the two together, and made one kind of synthesis in the country houses, and another and a more exalted one in the cathedrals. They did indeed offset Pan with the Christian God, but the houses of this God could never be a mere northern replica of the Roman basilica. The forests influenced them until the cathedrals became as mysterious as the dark woods. Between them they show two faces of the same civilization.

Today the cathedrals have travelled even farther towards the forests, and become more truly their complements. All the known and unknown dangers, all the fears and ferocities which once lurked in the forests have now migrated to human communities. No peril is more dire than that under which city people live, and no uncertainty and restlessness more intolerable. So men now go to the forests in search of peace and sanity, and freedom from terror. In India for centuries the forests have been giving shelter to the peasants whenever they are threatened by oppression or anarchy. In the West they are providing shelter from a disquiet which has become normal and quotidian.

Thus it happened that I could find the peace of the woods more readily in contemporary Europe, in spite of its industrialization, than in agricultural India. Even in Rome, where the urbanism of the Mediterranean world is felt in all its continuity in history and at its greatest sophistication, I could reach the woods after an easy walk from my hotel near the Pantheon. As I looked on the Borghese Gardens from the Villa Medici they suggested to me the peace of my Himalayan resort.

So the cathedral and the forests and fields have come to form one landscape in Europe, and they have come together more closely today than they ever did in the past.

VII

THE MOTHER CITY OF THE AGE

IT IS GENERALLY THOUGHT natural that the reality should fall short of expectation, especially with a man who has read a good deal about the things he is seeing. In such circumstances it has become almost a point of good manners to ask, 'Are you disappointed?' This question was often put to me in England. Fortunately, I was also able to combine truth with politeness in answering it. For one thing, I always find every bit of reality more interesting than the most effusive romanticizing about it. I was never disappointed with the Taj Mahal, as almost all clever people are. Next, in actual fact, the English scene seemed much more romantic to me than all the descriptions of it in poetry.

But when I saw this scene my conception of it came to be formed on a principle which was different from an Englishman's. It appears to me that in their love for their country Englishmen are like Kipling. They evidently share his feeling that although God has given them all England to love, since men's hearts are small, He has also ordained that for each man one spot should be the most loved of all. Kipling's spot was Sussex, and I have heard equally strong preferences expressed for the other counties.

My case was different. I was a foreigner, and as such all aspects of the English scene had the same charm for me. These also contributed to the formation of a conception of the whole in which the parts were very consistent and strongly cohesive. In my mind all the features of the English landscape merged in one picture, just as the villages and the country houses, the towns and the cathedrals also formed one composition. I did not indeed see the more mountainous parts of the north, which people say are quite different from the tranquil south, but I do not think that if I had seen them my impression of a general harmony in the English scene would have been disturbed. So what happened with me was that instead of reducing the idea of England to one concrete particular, as Englishmen tend to do, I fused the details into a general idea and sentiment. All English landscape appeared very much alike to me. It also evoked a consistent mood.

There was, however, one tremendous exception, which was not the industrial landscape, though. The traditional landscape in England, that is to say, the appearance of the country built up through the centuries down to the Industrial Revolution, is still the English landscape. The industrial age has not yet created any landscape properly so called, though it has scarred the previously created one. It may indeed be that all over the West the industrial civilization is making a beginning in this respect. It seems to have become conscious that it too must think of appearance, if not quite like a woman, at all events in the manner of a man. But the full outcome of this remains to be seen.

I shall have a few words to say on what I felt about the inroads of industrialism into the English scene, as well as its promise of better conduct, in connection with the contemporary situation of the English people, for the topic belongs to the present moment of their history, and has not as yet taken its place in timeless England. The exception about which I was going to speak has done so, and it is, of course, London. It is more of the present and the future than of the past, and it takes its place quite naturally in the Age of Science, though it had acquired a distinctive personality before the coming of the Industrial Revolution. In this, London is like modern capitalism, which belongs to the industrial order, and yet was created in the pre-industrial era.

For me, all through, London stood out vast, stark, and powerful, against the rest of England. If I were a Marxist, I should have said that if the traditional landscape was the thesis in human geography built up by history, London was the antithesis brought into being by the same historical process, and I do not know whether a synthesis will follow.

I suppose the great industrial cities would go with London. I did not see any of them with the exception of Birmingham, and that only very cursorily. It struck me, at all events visually, that Birmingham was a replica of nineteenth-century London. I think I can count it and also its fellows among the offspring of London, and the Great Mother of modern cities has many children both in the West and the East. I include Calcutta among them.

London has always been thought of as very special. In *Chamber's Encyclopaedia* I find a quotation from William Dunbar, who wrote at the end of the fifteenth century, 'London, thou art of townes *A per se*.' I do not know what exactly made him write that. But in any case, by the eighteenth century, the word *town* used without any article had come to mean only London, so that no one had to explain what town he had in mind if he said that someone was going to or was out of town. Perhaps London is more exceptional today than it ever was before. I felt it as I was coming from the airport, though I did not understand what caused this sensation in me.

London is big and complex, and most visitors get lost in it, not only physically but also intellectually. Even the Londoner does, for he very often speaks only of particular features of London, and shrinks from summing it all up. He says that London has never been planned or even built, it has grown. He would even be proud to add that it does not possess any obvious beauty of appearance, it has not acquired any form that can be easily captured by the eye, being more or less inchoate; one has to live in London to sense its personality; a man might spend a lifetime in it making daily discoveries, and yet his discoveries would not end; so you have to accept London in parts.

This is so obviously true that most foreign visitors just ignore the formlessness of London, or, if they are clever, air a kind of cynicism over its untidiness. I had heard so much of it from my countrymen who had been to England that when I actually saw London I was quite surprised to find that it was much more tidy and orderly than I had thought it would be. I oriented myself very easily there with the help of the axis furnished by the continuation of Bayswater Road into Oxford Street, and of Oxford Street into Holborn.

The cynical vein was really started by English literary men. Byron wrote:

A mighty mass of brick, and smoke, and shipping,
* Dirty and dusty, but as wide as eye*
Could reach ... a wilderness of steeples peeping
* On tiptoe through their sea-coal canopy;*
A huge, dun cupola, like a foolscap crown
On a fool's head —and there is London Town.

That was written not long after Canaletto had painted the Thames in London. What would Byron have thought today?

Less gifted people try to get round the overpowering vastness and variety of London by sampling it. I also did, to begin with. I looked for its beauty spots.

Although it is not usual, or fashionable either, to speak of the beauty of London, I would repeat that it has its beauty spots, St James's Park, for instance. I thought it was the most charming city park I had seen, and I do not go back on that opinion even after seeing the Tuileries Gardens and the Luxembourg. From the suspension bridge I saw a view which took my breath away. In a book of photographs by Helmut Gernsheim I had seen that view, but I was never quite convinced of its faithfulness. There seemed to have been some photographic manipulation to secure the effect.

But the photograph was absolutely realistic, as I discovered from the bridge. There was the same view before me, the same transparent mist, the same domes and cupolas, and the same toning down of the architectural masses. With the exception of the Banqueting Hall, Whitehall itself is stodgy. Indeed so successful was it in giving a consistent and thoroughgoing impression of heaviness that I had some difficulty in finding its famous architectural masterpiece. I overlooked it completely, going down from Trafalgar Square towards Westminster, and, feeling very ashamed, walked up again, noting every building until I came upon it. But from the bridge in the park Whitehall looked transformed. It became capable of suggesting not only the château of Chambord, from which the architect is said to have copied the skyline, but even the Kremlin. It looked so dreamy, aerial, and exotic that it was not difficult to imagine that Ivan the Terrible, or his latterday successor, Stalin the Terrible, was ruling from it.

There are innumerable other beauty spots to be seen in London. I also tried a second method of sampling it—looking at its historical monuments and scattered gems of architecture. Both the Norman and the Gothic style can be admired in London in detail, if not as complete wholes in their proper setting, as in the cathedral towns. Henry VII's Chapel is one of the most beautiful Gothic interiors I have seen, though it might not produce the same mood of spiritual elevation as the naves at Winchester and Chartres. I was glad to escape into it from the Abbey itself, which to my thinking was sadly spoilt by the white marble funereal sculpture. I would have denied every son of Britain, however great, that kind of honour and homage to save the Abbey from this vandalism.

As regards classical architecture, London has St Paul's. After seeing both Paris and Rome, I would not concede that anything in these two cities surpasses St Paul's for massive beauty and symmetry. It is the supreme manifestation of English classicism in architecture, rivalling the great achievements of classicism in literature, and putting to shame its tawdry expression in sculpture.

I also tried to see London in the way I did Paris. I stood on Westminster Bridge, wondering if it had a clearly felt facade. Certainly, there was a very impressive river front from the Houses of Parliament to St Paul's. It took form, but only a form that suggested power, and not architectural harmony. The other bank crystallized into nothing, in spite of County Hall, Lambeth Palace, and what was then the latest addition, the Royal Festival Hall. I also contemplated the river. Most definitely it was not part of the architectonic of London. It was a waterway, attractive at a few points, ugly at some, and plain for the greater part. But at certain times and in certain lights it can become transfigured. I saw this once, and I shall never forget the scene.

As a sort of overture, I saw the Thames from the huge foyer of the Festival Hall. A kind of Diwali, the Hindu light festival, seemed to be on, and then, as I walked back to my hotel, I saw the whole north bank from Waterloo Bridge. It was very quiet, and a keen breeze was blowing, making the atmosphere crisp and clean. Before me was Somerset House, softly floodlit, and standing out as it never does in the day. The dome of St Paul's was also illuminated, and so were the towers of the Houses of Parliament. For once the river and the city had become one. I had just heard the Second Symphony of Beethoven, for me the first live performance of a work which on records had been familiar for something like twenty-five years. Its lovely slow movement has never ceased to be a wonder to me. Tovey has written about it that 'to many a musical child, or child in musical matters, this movement has brought about the first awakening to a sense of beauty in music'. This was literally true of the child in Western music that I was in my early thirties. The themes were still in my ear, and they supplied a musical accompaniment to the luminous vision on which my eyes were resting.

Yet I am perfectly sure that not one of these ways is the right one to see London qua London, not only of our days but also of the eighteenth century, the London of which Dr Johnson said that to be tired of it was to be tired of life. In order to feel how true this dictum is and to understand the meaning of London as a centre of human life in our times, one must see it as a whole. It is curious that the great Londoner should also be the man to point that out.

'Sir,' he said, 'if you wish to have a just notion of the magnitude of this city, you must not be satisfied with seeing its great streets and squares, but survey the innumerable little lanes and courts. It is not in the showy evolutions of buildings, but in the multiplicity of the human habitations which are crowded together, that the wonderful immensity of London consists.'

I discovered that soon enough. After being able to find my way about in central London or rather the West End during the first few days of my stay, I acquired a wholly false confidence, and thought that I had mastered the city. A very disconcerting experience was to follow. On the fourth day after my arrival I was going to Canterbury by car, and when it passed by the Elephant and Castle I sat up, expecting to see the built-up areas thinning out and the famous English countryside making its appearance. But as we sped on, the unending blocks of buildings became more and more solid, and I was not sure that I had left London behind even when we had passed through Bromley. I am not familiar with the topography of Greater London, and I cannot say whether I was not going along one of those ribbons which are the tentacles by means of which London clutches the countryside, but even the main bulk of Greater London was crushing enough.

My experience was similar when I motored out to the north. On that side, however, I saw an additional belt. I passed along a vista of detached buildings, which were remarkably alike, and stood in immensely long rows like uniformed soldiers on parade. Red roofs, pink or cream walls, white windows, porches, little garden plots, following one another in endless succession, looked like a string of beads held together by the unbroken road and pavement. My English companion identified the houses sometimes as mid-Victorian, sometimes as late Victorian, sometimes as Edwardian, and did not seem to be wholly happy about them. I thought that this must be the famous Suburbia, on remembering which the intellectuals and aesthetes shudder and grow grey with fear. I did not, however, see much harm in the houses, for I was used to the suburbs of Calcutta and Delhi. None the less, I learned that beyond the London of history, and of my previous knowledge, there was another London, of whose immensity and mass, gravitation and power, I was totally unaware.

This impression becomes stronger, almost nightmarish, if one goes out of London by train from one or other of the main stations. I did so from Paddington, Euston, Liverpool Street, Charing Cross, and Waterloo. I shall never forget those journeys. The train seemed to cut through the living but grey and grimy flesh of the city, exposing backyards, clothes-lines, peeled-off plaster, kitchens, bathrooms and coal-heaps, in its desperate anxiety to break out into the countryside, where it was more at home and could breathe more freely. I had seen something like this in Calcutta, but was wholly unprepared for the scale on which it was exhibited in London.

Once I saw a very unexpected and bizarre spectacle behind this townscape. Suddenly, there appeared above the untidy tiers of brickwork a forest of derricks and cranes, suggesting water and a crowded port. At the time I could not make out what exactly that meant, but later I found out that I was passing south of the Pool.

It was in these comings and goings that I formed a truer idea of the structure and function of London than I could have done by merely seeing its sights. But it was an idea which was opposed to that which might have been arrived at by reading its history— that London might be loose and straggling because it had expanded from the nucleus furnished by the City or Westminster, swallowing up village after village in its haphazard growth. On the other hand, whatever loose spaciousness is to be found in it, lies at its core—the Royal Parks, the gay West End, and the City, silent and deserted at night. If one had to estimate the difference between Pitt and Addington today from Canning's famous quip, 'Pitt is to Addington, as London is to Paddington,' none would be likely to be felt.

After seeing London I have discovered at least one of the reasons for which my countrymen prefer to travel in it by the Underground. It is not simply that they want to go about quickly and without physical effort, or to reduce the sense of distance; they must also wish, subconsciously at all events, to escape the incessant and oppressive bombardment of the spirit by the brickwork of outer London. Astronomers say that the earth grows denser from layer to layer towards the centre; here it is a case of the clanging nickel and iron being in the thick crust.

I am sure that if I had had to live continuously in London, I should have been crushed. Even as it was I felt overpowered, although I spent half the time in the country. The exhaustion did not come merely from the lack of spaciousness. I did not feel what I felt in parts of London in the narrow Rue du Bac of Paris, or in the Corso in Rome, or even in the labyrinthine quarters around the Piazza Navona or Palazzo Farnese there. The oppressive sensation came not only from the houses, but also from the apparent quality of the life lived in these parts. I did not get it in Brook Street. Anyhow, the feeling remained so strong that after my return, when I sent one of my sons to London for his education, I tried to secure accommodation for him near Hyde Park, and finally felt very happy to have him fixed up north of Hampstead Heath, not very far from Ken Wood.

But I cannot allow my personal inclinations and lack of robustness to influence my opinion about the proper method of understanding London, which must be seen in its total functioning, rather than in its history and architecture. Very soon I became aware that there was a Greater London of the spirit as there was one of administration. That London gave a sensation of throbbing power and vitality, in spite of wearing a thoroughly workaday look. This is felt very strongly in the outlying parts, Hammersmith or Camberwell, especially on a Saturday afternoon.

London must be regarded as the base of a new mode of human existence, and that is what it has been in the last hundred years or so, and is today. It is a town which has broken out of the old classification of human habitations as rural and urban. It is no longer a historic city, although it has a long history. London is neither Westminster Abbey, nor the Tower, nor Lincoln's Inn Fields, nor St Bartholomew-the-Great, not St Paul's, nor Chelsea, nor even nineteenth-century Whitehall. Also, it is not of the Roman times, nor of the Middle Ages, nor of the Renaissance, nor of the Augustan Age, although it has monuments from every epoch. In spite of being overwhelmingly Victorian in appearance, it does not belong to the Victorian age as Paris belongs in some measure to the age of Baron Haussmann. It has absorbed all its past, near and distant, in its present.

Paris, on the other hand, gave me the impression that it was always hanging at a point of time, in spirit even when not in form, whatever the date of its buildings, and that it was assimilating its present to a particular period of its history. It was like a château in which successive generations of owners were installing all the modern devices of comfortable living without destroying the historic character of the place. I felt this as soon as I went to Paris from London, and wrote to my people:

'The more I see of Paris the more I feel that it belongs entirely to the past. The only modern or ultra-modern thing in Paris is the motor traffic. In every street you feel as if you were in an aeroplane. But the cars move so fast—you do not see anything but a blur when they pass you—that they become projectiles and completely impersonal. So Paris looks, though it does not sound, as a thing of the past. Perhaps we shall have to go to Donzére-Mondragon or the Régie Nationale des Usines Renault to see modern France. As for the Eiffel Tower, this monstrosity, which throughout the world has become the symbol of Paris, is completely out of keeping with everything else in the city. It is a blotch left by the industrializing nineteenth century on the sixteenth-to-eighteenth-century landscape of Paris.'

At the time I did not know that another monstrosity was to rise in the same quarter. It is the new Unesco Building, a typical product of the twentieth century, which appropriately reflects in architecture the shallow, insincere, and sterile international-ism of our times. The nineteenth century was at least fecund.

London does not need such a building, not even its Festival Hall, to be modern. It is modern by virtue of being the first and archetypal city of our age, created by modern government, bureaucracy, finance, world empire, international commerce, and industrialism. It is modern also by virtue of the great fear under which it lives— that of annihilation with all its inhabitants. It is the Mother Megalopolis of our era, with a family in every part of the world, where the things which have created it are also to be found. I have already said that Calcutta is one of its children.

I have written about Calcutta, and after living in it for thirty-two years I thought I understood it. When, however, I came to live in Delhi the difference between the two cities began to puzzle me. Delhi with all the other cities of northern India seemed to belong to an urban family which was completely different from that of Calcutta. It was only after seeing London that I discovered the true lineage of that city. It was a half-caste offspring of London, whereas the northern Indian cities were descended from the Islamic and pre-Islamic cities of the Middle East.

When I spoke about the power and modernity of London an American friend smiled. I am familiar with that smile. It lights up the faces of our very modern young ladies when one speaks of the modernity of their mothers, who were born around 1900. The sleek, streamlined and facile modernity of these girls is not to be compared with the modernity of the mothers, which was vital, weighty, struggling, and uneven. But while the previous generations have begotten, the new generations remain barren, however fully they may be living for and by themselves.

London's modernity is old-fashioned, but it is still living and creative. It is old but it has not ceased to grow. I am sure that even now it has not taken its final shape, and it is not possible to foresee what it will ultimately be. To me the greatest wonder about London is that it is historical and young at the same time, illustrating the process of evolution of the modern city besides being one of its most notable products. I may be a man of the past, unable to accept the wholeness of London, but I am not so narrow as to underestimate its stupendous role and overlook its gigantic presence.

PART II

The English People

I

WHAT DO THEY LOOK LIKE?

THOUGH I AM GOING to speak about the English people now, I do not intend to offer even the sketchiest of psychological studies. To try to do so after seeing them for *only five weeks* would be like attempting to write the biography of a man after meeting him at a cocktail party. My acquaintance with the English people had no chance really of becoming deeper. In fairness to me it should be remembered that my account is concerned with the superficies of English life, though it might be claimed, even without solving a difficult metaphysical question, that appearance does in some measure correspond to reality. But perhaps some of the most basic things are just those commonplaces which are always meeting the eye, and for that precise reason as frequently evading the mind.

To give only one example. Neither in London nor in the country was I able, by looking at the faces, figures, and clothing of the people, to guess that there had been invasions of England and spells of foreign rule for its inhabitants. In respect of India, this is one of the easiest of things to do even in one street in Delhi. From the verandah of my house in Nicholson Road I can see, first, the representatives of the aborigines of India, to whom the country belonged in the earliest ages; then the descendants of all the invaders, the Aryans, Scythians, Huns, Muslims, and British; and last of all the Indian minority created by British rule, standing out from all the rest by reason of their clothing. All of them are distinguishable from one another. But I could never make out a Celt, Roman, Saxon, Dane, or Norman in Oxford Street. If one has to understand a people I do not think that such trifles can be ignored, though they may not readily engage the mind.

But however casual my acquaintance with the English people, I should have been able to illustrate what I have to say about them by reproducing conversations. Here I created a difficulty for myself through my own behaviour. Even when I had opportunities for meeting Englishmen, some of them very distinguished, I did not allow them to talk, but talked all the time myself. What I was seeing in England was making such an impression on me that, though neither dying nor drunk, I was incessantly babbling of green fields and suchlike. On the other hand, if the conversation turned on things Indian, holding very strong views on them, I inflicted endless harangues on my hearers. Many of them noticed this loquacity and were very much amused by it.

I was not so naïve, however, as to remain completely unconscious of what I was doing, and that at times vexed me. The student of English manners in me was able to see how un-English I was being and at the same time I was too much what I was to succeed in checking myself. Anticipating such a situation, I had, immediately after my arrival, sought the advice of my young friend from the B.B.C. who was to act as my keeper in London. I told him that I was unused to English social conventions, and asked him whether it would do if I were to behave naturally instead of trying to think out what the correct English behaviour was, and being constrained and artificial as a result. He approved. But it was one thing to lay down the general principle of naturalness, and quite another to decide in each particular case what would be accepted as natural in me by Englishmen. So the upshot was, as we fatalists of the East say, what was bound to happen happened.

Besides, during my stay, I did not feel at all like an earnest enquirer after truth, who had been given an assignment to find out quickly and infallibly what was taking place inside England. If I might venture to offer an opinion on this popular method, there is no better one of arriving at untruth. I had indeed agreed to write a few talks for the B.B.C., but even when reminded I steadily refused to discuss or even think about them. I did not feel like a tourist either, and by the time I had reached England I had forgotten the names of the things I had planned to see. I was resolved to go about like a man visiting the houses of his friends, where many things were to be seen and learnt, but where what is now called reportage would have been an unforgivable offence and the loose-leaf notebook an abomination.

For all these reasons my account of the English people will be an impression of their collective appearance and behaviour, larded with such remarks on their part as ultimately succeeded in reaching my ears and fixing themselves in my memory. Let me begin then with their appearance without more explanations.

I had been told that Englishmen belonging to the different social strata and professions were very different, not only in speech and behaviour, but also in their appearance, taking it as the sum of their features, figure, expression, and, of course, clothes. Therefore from the very first I was on the look-out for the class characteristics of this highly stratified society. On the morning after the day of my arrival I was walking through Hyde Park towards the Wellington Arch between half-past six and seven. I saw a small number of people there, some of whom were obviously passing through the Park on their way to work, and some working in it. Judged by their clothes they could have been anything from clerks to high officials in India, but I assumed that they were English workmen.

A little later, as I was approaching the Arch, I saw another man coming from the direction of Park Lane. He was certainly different, for he was tall and slim, had a face which was thinner than that of the others, and on this face too there was a wider range of complexion, the forehead and certain parts being almost white, and the check-bones and the tip of the nose pink. He was also dressed in better clothes, and was wearing a blue overcoat rather negligently. I am afraid I gave the impression of staring at him, because I was revolving in my mind whether he could be a denizen of the famous Mayfair, come to recover from the dissipations of the night. Of course, even now I do not know if the inhabitants of Mayfair are capable of taking the air in Hyde Park between six and seven in the morning on March 29.

At Hyde Park Corner I saw people who seemed to be intermediate between the exceptional person I had just seen and the others in the Park. They were in no way remarkable. But when after loitering for some time I reached the corner of

Great George Street and Parliament Street, I saw a very striking apparition—a tall, well-built man in a neatly pressed dark overcoat, wearing a bowler hat and holding an umbrella in his hand. He looked like a Cabinet Minister of my conception, but was not walking with the long strides which I had seen them taking when going down to the House, in the pictures in the illustrated papers. This man was walking slowly, almost absent-mindedly. 'Must be an agent of the New Tyranny—an English civil servant,' I said to myself. As I walked on farther, more bowler hats and umbrellas began to make their appearance, and I was able to discover that there were bowler hats and bowler hats, and umbrellas and umbrellas, which piece of observation enabled me later to buy a really good umbrella, although to my great regret I could not acquire a bowler hat.

Exercising my faculties of observation in this manner I became able within a few days to guess the station in life and class affiliations of a fair number of Englishmen, though my perception of these differences could go nowhere near the native's. I could see that the professions did contribute to the external appearance and behaviour, and that a civil servant was not quite like a don. But to my thinking they showed many more common traits than differences. They all conformed to what to my unpractised eye seemed to be the upper middle-class type, to be distinguished from the lower middle-class, which I could also recognize. Lastly, I could also make out the workman type.

Yet all the differences that I was able to detect, and which are great by Western standards, fell far short of what I was used to in my country, where the variety needs no observation but literally *saute aux yeux*. This will be considered natural because India is more a continent than a country, has many languages and regional cultures, and is, so to say, a U.N., or even a Dis-U.N. like the real U.N., rather than one nation. All this is true but still not an adequate explanation. It does not account for the very wide range of variety that exists even within one culture group within one province, where one can find greater variations in dress, to speak of only one kind of difference, than in the whole multi-continental area from the Urals to California. It does not explain why after taking over the European male dress the anglicized upper middle-class in India, which forms a very small section of the population and is very homogeneous in other matters, has already evolved about a dozen variations of it, working out all the permutations and combinations, omissions and inclusions, of its separate components. To this particular kind of differentiation even the Government of India has made an official contribution by introducing a new coat after Independence. To give yet another example, in England the politicians, including the Ministers, and the officials are clad in the same manner. In our country there are two standard dresses for the politicians and two for the officials, all derived from separate culture complexes, and minor variations are appearing even within these. The mere size of the country could not have brought about this heterogeneity, deeper forces must have been at work.

If I were inclined to be philosophical I should have said that Nature imposes on every people a severe penance for the system of philosophy it creates. Thus we Hindus who have propounded the philosophical system of the Vedanta, which denies changes and bids us to seek salvation only in the formless Absolute, are driven in our actions to proliferate variations in the most patently biological manner, but the Westerners who have put forward the theory of evolution have to do everything in their power to approach the undifferentiated Brahma. But certainly this is far-fetched, and in any case I am no metaphysician. So I would look for an explanation of the greater range of difference that we show in more matter-of-fact circumstances.

It would seem that climate and weather have shaped different modes of exercising individual liberty in the East and the West. Living in the tropics we like to relax, lose control of our appearance and behaviour, and thus create differences through our failure to keep to the track. The people of the West are braced up by the cold to exercise greater will-power in casting themselves in a uniform mould. Lush growth in the tropics is not a phrase which applies only to vegetation.

However that may be, I failed to see in England one great distinction which is basic in my country. When I was there I was always asking myself, 'Where are the people?' I did so because I was missing the populace, the commonalty, the masses, or, if I may use a military term, the other ranks as distinct from the classes.

In India, on the other hand, wherever we go we notice two kinds of people, the ordinary folks who dress in their own way, that is both traditionally and scantily, speak their own dialects, behave in their own way, without sophistication and without affectation, as against the minority who wear the older Hindu or Muslim aristocratic costumes, speak both English and the standard forms of the Indian languages, and have what in the West would be called a middle-class pattern of behaviour.

This distinction has suggested an image to my mind. Our society seems to me to be like a ship which has a large black hull and a white superstructure. In England I did not find the hull. The people seemed to be all superstructure, all saloon, upper-deck and bridge.

When I spoke about this to the head of an educational institution in the East End, he observed that it was partly a matter of dress, for in a cold country everybody had to wear a certain amount of clothing, and that gave an impression of uniformity. No doubt he was right, because the distinction between the classes and the masses, which I did not see in England, is felt in the first instance in India on account of the bareness of the body. None the less there must be other reasons as well. The uniformity was clearly a recent creation, and the latest social changes have certainly made a substantial contribution to it.

Now I must record a different set of impressions about the appearance of the English people, which will seem not only ungracious but also unintelligent. Nevertheless I shall set them down in all honesty. My eyes (O my poor eyes!) could see very few beautiful and fashionably dressed women. The comparative rareness of beauty puzzled me so much that I more than once asked my friend from the B.B.C., 'But where are your beautiful women, whom of old the painters painted and the poets raved about? Where are they to be seen?' 'Why, in the streets,' he replied to my astonishment. As regards fashion, I saw an immense number of beautiful dresses in the shop windows, some displayed by themselves, others on the lifeless models. But I missed the living counterparts of the latter. The majority of the women seemed to be in very ordinary clothes, so far as I could judge.

After some time, however, my eyes began to acquire the faculty of picking out fashionably dressed women. But towards the beginning the working women appeared to me to be the more obviously chic, so I asked the wife of a friend, who had lived for some time in India, 'How does it happen, Mrs M—, that in your country the chambermaids seem to be much more smart than the *mem-sahibs*?' 'Because the chambermaids have been getting richer and richer, and the *mem-sahibs* poorer and poorer,' was her prompt reply.

Some days later her husband was driving me through the West End, and he suddenly asked, 'Mr Chaudhuri, you have now seen people of the upper middle-class, and people of the intellectual type, but have you met fashionable people, who live about here (he waved his hand towards the west and south-west), who are busy the whole day and yet do nothing? For instance, a person like that....' He looked up from the wheel, and turned his eyes in the direction of a lady who was standing on the opposite footpath. I scrutinized the Mayfairienne, but could not discover anything very special, although the distinctiveness of the man in Hyde Park had been easily seen by me.

At the next stage of the training of my senses, I began to notice that some women were dressed in a manner which suggested the fashion plates I had seen, and the realization came first with the sight of a lady in a very large hat, whom I saw at Stratford-upon-Avon, where I had gone for Shakespeare's birthday celebrations.

Finally, only two days before I left England, I saw a whole bevy of fashionable ladies at a reception in the house of a European diplomat, to which I had been invited. It was as if, with the coming of spring, they had burst into bloom overnight like the azaleas and rhododendrons I had waited so many weeks to see. Yet I must confess that these beautiful and smartly dressed women pleased me more in the manner of well-designed motor-cars than as women.

Shocking as it may sound, I have yet another confession to make. Paris struck me as being even more ordinary than London in this respect. The women appeared to be plain and dowdy, and there was the same contrast between the shop-windows and the world of living women. It was only in Rome that I saw a fair number of pretty women going about in the streets. The north seemed to have made a hidden treasure of its beauty and fashion to me. Since for something like two years before I went to Paris I had been handling a large number of photographs of the creations of the Parisian *haute couture* I was very much surprised by what I actually saw.

But I could not leave it at that. After thinking long over the subject I have found that the impression I formed was due to my way of seeing, which was conditioned by a whole series of antecedent circumstances, and had nothing to do with the reality. I shall set down these circumstances *seriatim*, without making any distinction between my purblindness in regard to beauty and to fashion.

In the first place, we who live in the tropics are susceptible to the texture and colour of cotton and silk, but cannot easily detect the elegance of woollen garments, and as it happened I was in England too early in the year for the women to have shed their winter coat to go into their summer plumage, which was on display in the windows. Besides, it must be said that there is some difference between the winter coat of animals and that of women. A silver fox or an ermine is much more resplendent in winter than in summer, but with the women it is the opposite.

I am sure that the ladies of the West will forgive an Oriental's insensitiveness to their furry and somewhat otter-like elegance if I tell them that many of us do not see any beauty even in a leopard or a tiger, regarding both only as very strong and ferocious beasts. It was only after disciplining myself over years in zoological aesthetics that I was able to admire the roundness of a puma's tail or the grace of a polar bear's profile. But I did not stay long enough in the West to be able to extend my zoological sensitiveness to the human species, more especially to its female.

Secondly, in India physical beauty is largely associated with a fair complexion or what we regard as such, and this among a people who are generally dark attracts attention immediately. Moreover, the relatively dark faces reflect light unevenly, throwing the features into greater prominence. The pink Western faces send out, at least to our eyes, almost equal light from all points and surfaces, and thus the features tend to be flattened out.

Thirdly, the proportion of handsome women being somewhat low in India outside the Punjab, the women who are considered beautiful or consider themselves to be beautiful—the two categories not being equal in all respects—are very self-conscious. They never allow anybody to overlook them, and certainly they are more noticed than they should be not only for the good of their soul but even for that of their body.

Fourthly, the relatively dark complexion makes lipstick, rouge, and other aids to natural beauty more obtrusive than on the faces of the Western women, where they appear to merge in the natural appearance of the face and thus lose their power to draw attention.

Fifthly, all women in India, and more especially those who have pretensions to fashion, have the habit of overdressing. They will go out in the morning dressed as if for a dinner, and there is no time of the day which is not jewellery time for them. Some even rush into their dressing-rooms if a casual visitor arrives, and do not show themselves until they have renovated themselves from head to foot. It is an open question, however, whether the visitor considers himself recompensed for the long vigil.

A man like me, who was used to this background of feminine beauty, was bound to have some difficulty in attuning himself to the wholly different style of beauty and display in the West. But in my case an additional personal factor was present. My idea of human physical beauty was derived almost exclusively from art. Therefore I had a fair amount of difficulty in appreciating it when it was not presented in the nude or in the historical costumes from the Renaissance to the eighteenth century. At the most the crinolines were my lowest limits. Therefore I think it will be understood why I thought that to-day there were no beauties in the West comparable to those to be found in painting or sculpture. For that very reason, again, the most glorious impression of human physical beauty that I brought away from the West was of its amazing nudes.

They remain in the foreground of my recollections of the visit. I looked for the pictures I had admired most in reproductions. I went in search of the beautiful *Rokeby Venus* of Velazquez in the National Gallery, and looked for Giorgione's *Concert Champêtre* in the Louvre. Ingres' *La Source* was not in its place, but I saw a version of it at Chantilly. The *Venus of Cnidus* by Praxiteles was also not on view in the Vatican Museum when I went there. But there were many others to be seen, and of course I saw the *locus classicus* of the nude in European art in the Sistine Chapel.

We Hindus too have a large number of nudes in art, and in its treatment have gone much farther in frankness than the Europeans, but the two unclad worlds are as different as the two draped ones. Perhaps I could illustrate this best by repeating an anecdote which I have heard. At Rome I had the good fortune to be able to see the Palazzo Farnese, which is probably the most beautiful of the Roman palaces. I saw the famous Carracci Room, and also another room with a very beautiful ceiling in carved cedar wood. A little boy, descended from one of the princely families, was showing the rooms to a visitor. He duly identified the figures in the painted ceiling as this or that notability of a bygone age, and then pointing to an ample female said, 'And that is my great-great-... grandmother.'

I do not think that any Hindu, standing in one or other of the great national galleries of the nude in his art, Konarak or Khajuraho, would care to point to one of the simpering ladies and say, 'That is my great-great-grandmother.' Hindu art has made it impossible to look at a nude without a leer, it has resolved flesh to its most fleshly elements, the Europeans have made it the expression of the spiritual in man. I have no wish, indeed I have no qualification, to join issue with any art critic who says that every kind of nude in art is erotic. All that I know is this: there are many forms of the erotic.

If anyone feels disinclined to believe me, he might go into the National Museum in Diocletian's Baths in Rome, and contemplate the *Venus of Cyrene*. She is only a torso, headless and therefore bereft of the seat of the spiritual in the human body, the face. But the amazing thing burns up all desire. Or he might look at the *Vénus de Milo*. As I contemplated her from all sides I thought it was legitimate to ask, '*Etait-elle en marbre ou non, la Vénus de Milo?*' She is no ordinary Venus, not the perilous goddess of Swinburne, not the evil blossom born of sea-foam and the frothing of blood, but the eternally beautiful mother, of whom sleeping children dream before they have learnt to dream of mates or mistresses. She is sister to the noble *Demeter* of the British Museum.

But what of Rubens? He is certainly a challenge to the view of the European nude I have put forward, and I never liked anything in him besides his magnificent technique. But I must give him his due, and I think that even with him one can say that he was only providing too much of a good thing, and not something inherently anti-spiritual. I could not remain insensitive to the staggering series in the Louvre which he painted for Marie de Médicis, and which now hang together in one room. I believe a better day will dawn for India if our politicians could allow themselves to be painted like that. I put the reason for thinking so in the partial obscurity of Latin: *nil cupientium nudus castra peto*!

The Eternal Silence Of These Infinite Crowds...

When visiting in England, I was almost always accompanied by an English friend, and, if not, I was furnished with introductions. Therefore the question of worming my way through the notorious English reserve did not arise in my case. I was not wholly reassured, however, by the easy clearing of the first hurdle, and feared that difficulties might crop up at a later stage, for among us in India the coldness comes after and not before the introduction. It is practised in the interest of a salutary peck order in the upper strata of our society. But in England I came across no chilliness or formality, and was never put in my place even by important people. I shall speak about this later. Here I am concerned only with the public behaviour of the English people.

Among us gregarious life is not just contented and speechless adjacence as among cattle and the English people, it is a demonstrative exhibition of kindliness as well as bad temper, accompanied by a good deal of sound. In India heartiness is found more in the public intercourse of men than in private social relations. Moreover, for us noise is as essential a condition of cheerfulness as is the warmth of the sun.

For this reason I was not surprised to read a very angry letter published in one of our newspapers shortly after my return from abroad, in which the writer, a countryman of mine, complained about the silent habits of the English people. He wrote with burning hatred of their behaviour in the Underground trains where they could think of nothing better to do than to bury their faces in their newspapers. A sailor perishing in the Arctic Ocean could not have felt more strongly about the icebergs.

I had heard about this habit before I went to England, but

to meet the silence at first hand was a wholly novel experience. To me it seemed that not even their forums and agoras could be associated with characteristic sounds. Life in London, even in the most crowded streets, seemed like a film of pre-talkie days. I had an uncanny sensation when I saw unending streams of people going along Oxford Street, and heard no sound. As they moved into the Underground stations they looked like long lines of ants going into their holes. When after living in the bazaars of India for years I saw a sight like that, it was only natural that I should paraphrase Pascal and cry out, 'The eternal silence of these infinite crowds frightens me!'

I met the same silence when, from the streets, I went into the pubs or restaurants. Both can be crowded at lunch time. But I heard no conversation. In India, on the contrary, such places would be buzzing or even booming with talk. Speaking of the clubs, though regarded as centres of social life, they are perhaps the most silent places of all. One evening, when dining at a club, I tried in my innocence to open a conversation across the table, and I admired the skill with which the intrusion was fended off without the slightest suggestion of discourtesy.

But Englishmen have heard so much about their habits of silence from foreigners that they will see nothing new in my experience. They have heard the comment mostly from Frenchmen and other Europeans, and so can have no conception of the contrast they present to our ways in India. It is this contrast rather than the general fact of the silence which I wish to bring home, and as it happens I am particularly qualified to do so, because never having had a car I have always travelled by bus or tram, than which there are no better places to observe the public behaviour of a nation. The transport system of Delhi, which is owned by the Government and in which I have gone about for more than fifteen years, is very illuminating in this respect.

In the buses of Delhi all of us make use of one another for bodily comfort. In northern India people have very great difficulty in keeping steady in moving vehicles, and therefore they lean against one another or put their arms round a fellow-passenger. Nobody is so ill-natured as to mind being used as a cushion, and if anyone with a wholly alien notion of private ownership in respect of his body objects, he is asked in offended tones, 'What harm is there in it, you are not a woman?' Again, if anyone wants to know the time and has not got a watch he simply takes up the left hand of another passenger and looks at his wrist-watch. I wear mine on the under side, and therefore I have my wrist twisted.

The buses are also full of conversation not only on public topics but also on embarrassingly private ones, and not only between acquaintances but also between people who have never met before. Among the former the jokes are loud and hearty, and they are also permissible between total strangers. One day a fellow-passenger looked at my large sola topee and remarked that it was heavier than my whole body, and when I replied that it was no bigger than his turban he said that he hoped I was not offended at his joke.

Another day I even had an anxious inquiry about my health. In the hot season I sometimes get an irritation at the back of my neck, especially because I wear a collar and tie even then, and this makes me jerk my head and even perk it like a bird. Last summer I had an attack of this and when travelling in the bus, I suddenly heard the gentleman sitting next to me asking me in English, 'Is it habit or is it disease?' As I was somewhat surprised by the question and could not at first understand what it was about, he repeated the query. I asked in my turn, 'What is habit or disease?' Then the gentleman mimicked me exactly and said, 'This.' I was bound in common politeness to reply, 'I suppose it is habit.' 'I thought so too,' he rejoined, 'You have done this too many times, and it has now become a habit, and habit as you know is second nature.' 'So it is, so it is,' I said in an embarrassed manner.

The passengers also help one another about the best way to get to a destination, because not infrequently the conductor has no clear idea of the topography of Delhi, and they often give contradictory directions, each maintaining that his is the right one. So far as newspaper reading is concerned, the fellow-passengers never snatch away anybody's paper, but they take the pages he is not reading, in the most polite manner, and distribute them among themselves. These are, however, scrupulously returned. Books are often tugged at. One day a fellow-passenger pulled hard at an edition of the Gita I was holding in my hand, and when I did not let go, but objected, he said angrily, 'You have got a holy book in your hand and you are behaving like this! I don't want your book.' And he did make a pariah of me.

I have the habit of leaving my seat and waiting at the door of the bus so as to be able to get down as soon as it comes to the stop, instead of keeping it waiting as most of us do. But when the others see me doing this, they cry out in their anxiety, 'Please have patience.' Some even catch hold of my coat-tails or grip the arm to prevent me from moving. They also help in more exceptional circumstances. One day I found that I had only one bad rupee with me, and the conductor would not take it. In such a situation it is the custom with us to appeal to the 'general will' of the passengers. As I did not do that a fellow-passenger snatched the coin from my hand, looked at it, and said, 'It is bad, but don't worry, I am going to exchange it for a good one.' And he took out a one-rupee note, gave it to me, and put my bad rupee in his pocket. I was so amazed that I could not prevent him.

All sorts of other incidents happen, which make the bus in Delhi a microcosm of our national life. On one occasion I saw a hysterical young woman trying to commit suicide by jumping out of a window, and being pulled back by her husband. There are quarrels, sometimes verbal, sometimes involving the limbs, not only between a passenger and another passenger, or a passenger and the conductor, but also between the conductor and the driver. One day the two quarrelled and came to blows, and then the driver got down in a huff and went off into Edward Park, to lie down on the grass. He did not come back until the whole body of passengers had shouted their entreaties to him for some time.

What takes place at the stops is even more out of the ordinary by Western standards, and I shall relate only one of my experiences. It should be remembered that in the capital of India the buses on certain routes come at intervals of twenty minutes or more, and that they are also irregular. I was waiting for my bus on one of these routes, and there came along an elderly gentleman with his family. He asked me if he could go to Red Fort from that stop, and when I said that he could, he thanked me profusely, and gave the information that he was a visitor to the town. He pointed to a young girl in the party, and said, 'That is my daughter, she is in her B.A. class, and I am thinking now of her marriage.' Then he introduced his son to me too. After that he went on to say that they were coming from the house of Pandit Jawaharlal Nehru, where they had his

Darshan, that is to say, were present at his ceremonial appearance before visitors. Continuing in this communicative vein, he informed me that the last time he had come to Delhi was two years ago, and that, he added with a shy smile, was over a lawsuit with his father.

I could hardly remain indifferent to the raising of such a topic. Seeing that I was interested he went to the trouble of explaining the whole affair. Of course, he spoke throughout in English, and I shall give his exact words so far as I can remember them.

'You see,' he began, 'my mother died some years ago, and my father, who was old at the time, took a concubine. My brothers and I did not mind this at all, but after some time he brought this lady into the house, which we could not pass over. So my brothers and I went up to him and said, "Revered Father, you cannot do that. You may, of course, associate with the lady, but you cannot bring her into our ancestral house where we, your sons, live with our children." Upon this my father got very angry and shouted, "Nothing doing! I shall disinherit the whole lot of you." We replied that he could not do that either. So it went to the courts. But the judge advised me to settle the matter out of court.'

At this point the bus came into view, and I prepared to move. The gentleman surprised me, however, by asking for my name and address. Upon my inquiring the reason, he replied that he wanted to send me some mangoes from his own orchard and that they were very good. I replied, 'Thank you very much. But there is really no occasion for it.'

'No, sir,' he rejoined with great warmth of feeling, 'it is no trouble whatever. You have given me the pleasure of your company and conversation, and I want to show my gratitude for it.' But the bus had come along and I had to jump into it, without being able to bring the matter to a more graceful conclusion.

It is this *comédie humaine*, this large-hearted wiping out of the distinction between public and private affairs, this craving for sympathy in widest commonalty spread, that make us recoil from the dreariness of the public behaviour of the English people.

III

IT ISN'T DONE

I SHALL NOW PASS on to the private behaviour of the English people. On this score my initial nervousness was somewhat relieved by a good augury, the courteous behaviour of the English cats. I was struck by this the very first morning. I observed that the stray cats which were going to their day-shelters did not slink down into the areas or take cover under the motor-cars, as they do in our country when they see a man, but walked on with *insouciance*, with a glance of mild curiosity at me. Soon they began to make direct overtures. At Canterbury, when I was walking among the ruins of St Augustine's Abbey, a cat came up and rolled on the path before me, in order to be picked up and tickled under the chin. When I did so it purred until I was ready to cry, thinking of the cordial state of Indo-British friendship in which I had never believed. At Penshurst Place another cat saw me from a door, and came walking right across the terrace to join me near the steps. When I scratched its neck, it followed me all around the formal garden. Then it met another very big cat and went off to gambol with this friend.

I was surprised by all this, because in Delhi I try to make friends with cats but receive no encouragement except from my own. When I mentioned this tameness to my English friends they said in their characteristic way, 'We are rather given to spoiling our cats.' Cats are, however, very good judges of the human character, and all nations get the cats they deserve. In England I found that even politicians were not undeserving of the compliment which the English cats pay by their behaviour to Englishmen in general. Politicians are an early love but late *bête noire* in my life, while cats are an early *bête noire* and late love. In England I found myself ready to love both at the same time.

I do not miss much in our politicians because I do not expect much, but in England I came to see that through this habit I might do serious injustice to the politicians of other countries. One incident made me take special note of this. I was at a big reception given by a diplomat in London. (Not ours, dear me! They are serious people, engaged in putting the world straight, who could not waste their time and attention on me. It was in the house of a European diplomat.) The rooms, hung with Gobelins tapestry, were beautiful, and they overlooked a fine park. They were full of very smart people, and as I sipped my champagne, I admired the decorations and the guests, particularly the ladies in their hats, which I had never before seen worn indoors.

Seeing me alone, a middle-aged Englishman came up with his wife and introduced himself, 'My name is L———, and this is Lady L———.' After a few words he asked me if I was a diplomat.

'Oh, no,' I replied, 'only a writer.'

'Why only?'

'I suppose in the company of so many diplomats a writer should have the modesty to say that he was only a writer.'

'No,' rejoined my acquaintance, 'it is I who have the right to the *only*. I am *only* a politician. I represent P——— in Parliament.'

Empty and insincere words? Yes, of course, who does not know that? But how much more pleasant than the heavy-footed sincerity and truthfulness to which I was used.

This leads me to think of the negative aspect of English behaviour, of which alone I shall speak here. In the universality of the parental habit of saying, 'Don't do this, that, or the other thing,' India exactly resembles England. If anything, Indian parents, with the exception of a minority who spoil their children thoroughly, are more addicted to saying No to everything proposed by the young people than any set of parents anywhere. But as regards the effect of the negative discipline no two societies could be more dissimilar. As soon as they are out of sight of their elders, our young people snap their fingers at them, and the guardians are too shy to notice the disobedience. In England, on the contrary, the latter succeed in making the negation stick, so that even the most rebellious young men acquire a formidable range of inhibitions from their elders. They become permanently incapable of doing many things which are done naturally by others— for instance, speaking French with a good accent when they have learnt to do so, working hard at school or university, discussing cultural or philosophical topics in company, and so on and so forth.

My son, who is at an English university and lives among English people, began to acquire this negative attitude very early, and in reply to various suggestions made by us often wrote back, 'It's *not done* here.' He put such an intensity in these simple words that I could almost see the ink blushing. Thus we were not at all surprised at what he wrote when I informed him that at a party in Delhi his mother had been heard talking about Chartres and St Peter's with a very eminent English art critic. He was very much interested but commented, 'Normally, in England, I would not do so as a topic of conversation.'

I shall give a few examples of this negative attitude from my own experience. On one occasion, talking with a distinguished English politician, I said that I was seeing England for the first time. 'Do you like it?' he asked, and when I replied, 'Yes, it is very lovely,' he observed, 'You are seeing it at a very favourable time.' Another Englishman, a writer, told me that I had been exceptionally fortunate in regard to the weather, and that had a great deal to do with my enthusiasm over the English scene. If I did not know how proud they were of the appearance of their country I should have thought that they were interested only in finding fault with it.

Another habit of theirs perplexes us, and at times causes social awkwardness. They do not disclose their position in the world. I have met distinguished people, but unless I knew who they were I should never have been able to guess that they had achieved anything at all. If they are authors they do not refer to their books, if they are thinkers they do not hold forth, if they are statesmen they do not disclose programmes for reforming the world, a man who is not well up in a subject might not be able to discover that an Englishman is an expert on it. This makes it difficult for us to decide how much civility to mete out to them.

I might refer in this connection to my experience with a very great English intellectual, whose name is known all over the world. He surprised me first by bringing in the tea himself and making it, then by not opening a discourse. He simply listened to what I was saying, putting in a word or two, and smoking a pipe all the time. I was not speaking on anything connected with his own interests — in fact, most of the time I was speaking about India — but his observations showed an amazing alertness of mind. He struck me most, however, by his reply to a remark of mine about a set of his own works, which I saw on the shelves. Going up to them, I observed, 'How beautifully they are bound!' He seemed to be rather embarrassed, and only said, 'They were presented to me by the Swedish Academy.' It was as if he wanted to apologise for his own works being on display and so well bound.

I shall now give another illustration of the same kind, but illustrating the attitude from the reverse side. When I was at the Adult Education Centre at Urchfont Manor in Wiltshire, the Warden told me that Mr Patrick Heron, an English painter, had come to lecture on art there. I asked him if he was the same Patrick Heron who had held an exhibition in London the previous May. 'You know about the exhibition, do you?' he said, 'You must be very clever.' I suppose the remark was intended to be a compliment, but I felt so confused that I replied that I had only read about it in *The Times*, meaning that I had only picked up the information accidentally and not collected it with the object of being an informed person.

Usually they keep their work and their social life separate. The only occasion in England when I found a man bringing his personal life and work together was at the house of a social worker in Bristol, with whom I spent a whole afternoon. He talked about his work, showed me his maps, explained his charts and statistics, and even read his case reports. But he was something of a crusader, and had been a pedlar in the streets at one time. His wife was of the normal type. She sat by us, knitting quietly, nevertheless her remarks, when she made any, showed that she was not only familiar with her husband's work and problems, but also interested in them.

Altogether, they live personally in the minor mode of music, and as it happens my son is acquiring this habit as well. Let me quote him again. He had met and talked with some compatriots after a long time, and he sent the following report to us:

'I was there for three hours, and came back terrified. For the first time I realized how far I had drifted away from my countrymen. They too felt it, and asked me many questions, trying to puzzle it out. In the first place, all of them talked in a way which seemed to me intolerable showing off by English standards. And then I saw that none of them were even aware of the qualities which I admire most in the English people. I said to myself, "Good Lord! If I, who after all am an Indian, can feel so remote from typical Indians, how distant must the Europeans feel." I am more convinced than ever that there can be no understanding between Indians and Europeans.'

I want my son to behave in Rome as the Romans do. As a matter of fact, before he left I impressed the necessity of this on him. But now I feel like telling the denationalized young man that when he comes back to us he must leave his new ideas west of Suez, if he is not to starve in India. Once I actually wrote to him in another connection that after teaching him to be a non-conformist in India I did not want him to become an English conformist, and I warned him most emphatically against Oxford and Cambridge. To push every advantage to the utmost comes naturally to us. We speak about them not only to those who might reward us for them, but also to those who have not got the same advantages. Thus among us, if a guinea-pig talks with a squirrel, whether the squirrel should or should not raise the topic of a tail is no question of social etiquette at all, it would be raised as a matter of course.

Nothing illustrates this attitude of ours better than our conventions of introducing a person. We usually pronounce a eulogium, and in any case emphasize the official position. In our society a man is always what his designation makes him, therefore we are very punctilious in giving it. At parties in Delhi I see people adding it themselves when the introducers omit to announce it. One day, at the house of a foreign diplomat in Delhi, a young man was introduced to me without his official position being mentioned. He immediately bowed and added, 'Of the X-Ministry, and what Department are you from?' When I replied that I belonged to none, he seemed to be as much surprised by the fact that I had been invited there at all as by my not having a designation.

On another occasion I heard a lady asking my wife, who had said that I was a writer, what I was before I was a writer. That rather reminded me of a cartoon I had seen in *Punch* of an East European with a pronounced Semitic nose, who had come to his solicitor to have his name changed. 'But you have already changed it once from Goldstein to Robinson?' said the lawyer. 'Yes, but nevertheless I want to change it again.' 'But why?' 'They ask me, "What were you before you became Robinson?".' The inquiry about me was in the inverse sense, groping from the unacceptable towards the acceptable.

I do not say all this in criticism of my people. Self-advertisement is forced on us by the urge for survival. The traditions of our society are such that a man is not credited with anything unless he can display it with effect. People who are endowed with the power to provide employment and recognition in India are incapable of seeing any merit in a man without having it dinned into their ears. These men cannot detect ability or talent. In fact, not to speak of human beings, they cannot recognize the signs of intelligence even in a fox-terrier. Most probably this statement will sound odd if I do not explain that even before I was thirty I had come to hold very decided views about the 'human face divine' as compared with the canine, and embodied the idea in an aphorism: 'In nine cases out of ten the movements and the looks of a dog betray intelligence, in nine cases out of ten a man's do not. Control over the facial muscles has made man look more stupid than he really is.'

However that may be, it is indisputable that our great men do not perceive talent, and therefore like regiments we have to carry our drums, and *tambourinage* is as essential a thing to the march of our careers as it is to the march of soldiers in the West. If anyone feels inclined to blame us for this I would ask him to consider whether he finds fault with the tiger for his roar, the peacock for spreading out its tail, and even with the caterwauling of domestic cats, unimpressive and unpleasant as it is compared with the other kinds of animal display.

I shall now consider some of the extensions and applications of this negative behaviour. I had gone down to Chislehurst to spend a day with an English couple, whose son I had known in India. The gentleman had heard that I was interested in birds, and so he said that he would take me out to do some bird-watching. We motored down to a gravel pit, which had become a lake. Taking me down to its edge, my friend only said, 'There.' I saw some ducks swimming, and on a small island a female swan sitting. The cob was swimming about, and keeping guard. All of a sudden one of the ducks approached him, and he chased it away. The duck dived but appeared again quite close to him.

He charged once more, and this went on for some time.

'You see,' said my friend, 'the mallard is very naughty, and it is teasing the swan.' He did not explain what a mallard was, and made no attempt to rub in the interest of the scene.

On our way back we were passing through the common. I looked at the bushes, on which I could see yellow flowers. 'These are...' I began.

'Gorse,' my friend replied without explaining what gorse was, and then went on to say, 'Let us see if there is any bracken.' He looked about him for some time, and said that there was not any, for it had not come out yet. He said nothing to explain bracken.

A little later he pointed to a monument and said, 'That is of interest today (it was April 16), for it is the monument to the man who introduced summer time.' After a while another monument came into view. 'That was erected to the Prince Imperial,' said my friend. No explanations here either.

The same sort of experience befell me at Cambridge. An elderly Fellow of King's College asked me, 'Have you seen the tapestry after Rubens in the hall?' I said that I had seen the hall but not the tapestry. He immediately took me there, climbed to the gallery in which it was hanging, and switched on the lights. Then he took me to the opposite gallery, from where I could obtain the best view of it. He left me entirely to myself. Incidentally, the tapestry depicted the Battle of Ponte Milvio, in which Constantine defeated Maxentius.

A similar thing had already occurred. The friend who was showing me Cambridge had taken me to the Combination Room of St John's College, and never told me what it was meant for, and though I used the phrase with a knowing air it remained like a thorn in my brain. So after returning to India I consulted my dictionaries, and came upon the following entry:

'Combination room = Common room. *Univ. of Cambridge.*' I felt relieved.

I shall give two more examples of the same kind. At Cambridge again, another friend inquired if I had seen the Gate of Honour at Caius, and learning that I had not he took me down to it. He also left me to contemplate it by myself. Another time, in Wiltshire, the friend who was taking me round suddenly turned the car away from the main road. When I looked at him with surprise he explained that he wanted me to see something.

Presently we came to a pretty village, and pointing to a section of the street, he said, 'That bit is quite unspoilt.' Nothing more, not a word to explain what *unspoilt* meant in that context, though the notion of an unspoilt place was so very English. The fact is that when an Englishman is friendly he imputes himself and considers all explanations as rudeness.

Certainly, Englishmen are not unaware of their habit of tacitness, which they call understatement. They are even proud of it, as if it was one of their titles to superiority over other nations, and overdo it at times. These other nations, however, take them at their word, and make no allowance for the understatement. At all events we Hindus as a rule do not see much in an Englishman. Not that we underrate his printed word. On the contrary, if we can learn about our country and ourselves from books written by Englishmen, we do not think it necessary to see the one and analyse the other. Even in regard to Hinduism most Hindus prefer to go to an English book. Only, we do not connect the book written by the Englishman with the English *man*. We do not believe in the biblical saying that every tree is known by its fruit, but gather what we take as grapes from what we despise as bramble.

Our forte being talking we do not readily perceive that the silence of the English people reserves their energies for work, and that to judge their real power of self-expression we have to see what they do and not simply hear what they say. Every nation has its peculiar manner of self-projection, and since the climate limits our capacity for work anyway, we would be foolish to forgo the advantage of talk. But we ought to be more willing to recognize an alternative way of self-expression and give the Englishman his due. In this he is now behaving more handsomely by us than we are doing by him. The gift of the gab, which the English people have always distrusted, seems now to exercise a spell on them when they meet it in us. They are fascinated by it and show themselves ready to credit us with as much genius as our talk seems to indicate in us. We show no appreciation of their negative traits.

We also fail to see how these — all their *Isn't Dones* — add up to a positive type of character, which in its physiognomy is like a subdued drawing in silver point, quite attractive to those who have a taste for such things. But the Englishman can also lay pastels, watercolour, and even oils on this sketch. Let me try to see how he does it.

IV

TELL ME THE WEATHER AND I'LL TELL THE MAN

THOMAS HARDY WROTE,

This is the weather the cuckoo likes,
And so do I;

I also would say, 'So do I.' I was in England in April, and
therefore the B.B.C. gave to my first talk, which was about the
English scene, the title, 'Now that April's there.' I did not,
however, find the season quite as Browning had described it,
although I stayed on till the beginning of May. That year spring
was late, the leaves less forward, and the birds less busy.
Nevertheless I liked it immensely.

This would seem unnatural to Englishmen and to my
countrymen, both of whom are in their different ways confirmed grumblers about the English weather. Indian parents
who send their children to England are as worried about it as
English parents who had sons in India used to be about our
snakes and tigers. So, when in my first letter to my family from
England, which was seven pages long and described the journey
and the arrival in detail, there was no mention even of the
weather, one of my sons wrote, 'We were expecting something
about the weather; I hope you will let us know whether it is too
cold or not.'

But I hardly gave any thought to it, taking it for granted.
In fact, I did not feel the cold at all. On the third day after my
arrival I was waiting for the bus at a stop opposite Hyde Park,
at about nine in the morning. A cutting wind was blowing, and
I had not taken my overcoat. An English lady who was there with

her little daughter looked at me and cried out shivering, 'Oh, how bitterly cold it is!' Perhaps the topic being the weather, she did not mind addressing a stranger and foreigner. 'Is it?' I asked quietly. 'You don't feel it?, she asked in her turn, and then she added, 'But you have brought so much sunshine with you.' That may have been the reason behind my insensitiveness, for it was not bravado. But my nonchalance did not outlast the day. By the afternoon I was nearly frozen and thought I should have to buy a bottle of cognac, of which I had seen some attractive brands in the windows. In my panic I actually bought a bottle of cod-liver oil, which of course I never took. In the end I recuperated on coffee, and by the time I went out again in the evening I had got back my aplomb and warmth, although at the time I did not know that I was going to dine on boar, peacock, and sillabub, and drink mead and flagons of mulled claret.

That was my only and shortlived quarrel with the English weather. Afterwards even continual rain, such as I had one day going about in Wiltshire, did not depress me. Another time I was caught in a spell of really squally weather. That was at Winchester. It spoilt my sightseeing, and also made me anxious about being able to catch the return train. But I thought I was compensated when I looked out, and again looked in, sitting near one of the great doors of the west front of the Cathedral and waiting for the storm to cease. All of it was so very English. There was driving rain, almost like sleet, and whistling wind; the trees were swaying violently; within a service was going on for the boys of the school after the main service, in which I had joined, was over. England was in a grave mood for me that morning, and what a place it was to watch that grave face from — the grand nave, soaring up even higher than it does on a sunny day, the stained glass shining dimly, the boys' choir, and the chanted words!

I do not deny, however, that the English weather can be very provoking, especially if one is intent on going about one's business. The distrust of the weather has been instilled into the English breast for all time. Whenever I spoke about my sightseeing, I was asked in anxious tones, 'Was the weather good?' I found this distrust embedded in a characteristic turn of speech. When in the Long Gallery of Hatfield House I was looking at the hat, gloves, and stockings of Queen Elizabeth I—

those she had left behind in her hurry to become queen—I suddenly asked, under the impression that she also had an umbrella with her, 'But where is the umbrella?' The elderly lady who was taking us round replied, 'She trusted to her luck.' However, she puckered her brows and said more to herself than to me, 'But when was the umbrella...?' 'Of course, in the eighteenth century,' I hastened to reply. The fact that the word *luck* is used in connection with the weather as with gambling appears to me to be significant.

Yet it was this capriciousness that I enjoyed most. Englishmen who complain about the unpredictability of their weather can have no conception how excruciating its predictability can be. Living in Delhi, for two months and more I cannot escape the certainty that the sky will be tawny, a heat haze will lie like a pall on the landscape, daylight will have a hard glare but no brightness, and the earth will look like dying of heat-stroke, as Kipling wrote.

My family came to Delhi at the beginning of a hot season, and after going through their first summer in northern India, became half-hysterical. So when, one evening towards the end of June, storm-clouds suddenly appeared in the sky, my servant whom I had brought over from Calcutta burst into the room, crying in a voice choked with emotion, 'Clouds, the clouds!' We left our dinner, and rushed out into the verandah. There were indeed clouds, piled up in black masses against the usual grey of the evening, with welcome flashes of lightning. It was as if we had gone through the siege of Lucknow, and heard the pipes of the Campbells.

My son, walking in the Mendip Hills in his first summer in England, remembered all this and wrote to us, 'I shall never forget it— the cows, the smell of hay, and farmyard; the grassy path with tall white flowers, red poppies, nettles, and honeysuckle—the English countryside we dream about. Have you read Rudyard Kipling's "At the End of the Passage"? All the time I was thinking about a conversation in it, which I still remember very well.

"Summer evenings in the country,— stained-glass window, — light going out, and you and she jamming your heads together over one hymn-book," said Mottram.

"Yes, and a fat old cockchafer hitting you in the eye when you walked home. Smell of hay, and a moon as big as a bandbox sitting on the top of a haycock; bats, —roses, —milk and midges," said Lowndes.

'Must have been terrible for those men to think about it all in June in India.'

It was this uniformity of our weather that made its changefulness in England so pleasant to me, and if you are once reconciled to it you really enjoy its mischief-making, and even its downright misbehaviour. I do not know why W.H. Davies in his poem on 'Leisure' did not include the weather among those things for which a man must have time, and did not say that it would be a poor life if he had not.

I think I have at last got a better understanding of the Englishman's grievance against his weather than even he has. To complain about it is a national pastime which has misled the world and led outsiders to give credit to the Englishman for attributes which he really owes to his weather. But before I speak about this I should like to observe that I think he really loves it, and that is why he is always quarrelling with it. Was it not La Rochefoucauld who said that if one were to judge love by the greater part of its effects it would seem to be more like hatred than friendship?

Now that there are so many means of protecting oneself effectively against bad weather, even children in England do not seem to be put out by it. On that rainy day in Wiltshire I saw a surprisingly large number of them out in the fields and walks. There were even babies in their prams, and toddlers swaggering along in their bright jerseys, caps and mackintoshes, unmindful of the fine drizzle. There were also a number of gipsy families resting by the wayside, the men and women sitting by the caravan, the children tumbling close by, and the horse grazing at a little distance, looking the most composed of the group.

Now to come to the main point. I think the weather has very largely entered into the formation of the Englishman's mind, and the training of his sensibilities. It has made him responsive to changes in the environment, capable of meeting surprises of all kinds, both pleasant and unpleasant, and of taking contretemps with good humour; above all, it has made him observant of and susceptible to concrete details.

I was very much intrigued by his absorption in small things. A boss, a knocker, a hinge, a paw foot to a chair, not to speak of a whole piece of furniture or a wrought iron gate, seemed to have an irresistible fascination for him. John Clare may have been a highly developed Englishman in his sensibility to small creatures, but unles he had been typically English he could never have written about the frog half-fearful jumping across the path, the little mouse leaving its hole in the evening and nimbling with timid dread beneath the swath, or the jetty snail creeping from mossy thorn with earnest heed and tremulous intent. I saw some of this interest in little things, and it seemed to lend an extraordinary zest to an Englishman's life.

In Wells cathedral I was buying some picture postcards, and my English companion picked up and tossed over one which showed a small figure in relief of *The Virgin of the Annunciation*, saying, 'You might take that, Mr Chaudhuri.' My own choice on the contrary was for the views of the whole building. At Cambridge, again, a very famous English writer asked me, when he heard that I had just been to the Fitzwilliam Museum, whether I had seen a little picture from a predella piece by Domenico Veneziano. As it happened, I had noticed *The Annunciation*, and even bought a picture postcard of it, but he was referring to another picture. So I went again and found it to be one which was quite familiar to me from a reproduction I had at home, but which I had quite unaccountably overlooked. It was the picture of *The Miracle of St Zanobius*.

The same characteristic is illustrated by the extraordinary sensitiveness that the English people show to the inherent attributes of wood, stone, metal or glass. They seem to be drawn by them as cats are by the texture of velvet and satin. We in the tropics would never have dreamt of leaving the beams exposed in a stately room like the Solar at Penshurst Place, or of putting a bronze bushel measure in it, even though it might have been cast from the guns of the Spanish Armada. An adzed beam would be resented by us as a symbol of racial discrimination if it could be seen in a room in which we had been put by an Englishman. We should not have noticed the slight waviness in the seats of the benches in the Marble Hall of Hatfield House, and we would not have affectionately held up and contemplated a piece in blue Bristol glass.

The interiors of the English houses, especially the great ones, also give evidence of the love of concrete details. They are in a way possible only in that climate and weather. They were made by and meant for a people who had to spend long evenings indoors, sometimes day after day, when the mind would be benumbed by its own emptiness unless it could crawl from one object to another along a continuous chain of interest — furniture, china, glass, plate, pictures, ornaments, fireplaces, and other fixtures. I was surprised to find how in the big private libraries of the houses, the books bound uniformly in leather and standing side by side were able to fix the attention individually, even before one had read the titles. These interiors were stocked on the same principle as squirrels' nests are in winter. Thus it happens that although most lavishly decorated they do not become oppressive or give an impression of overloading.

Such rooms would be unendurable in the tropics, where the light and wind have unhampered access to the interiors, and give to the mind an ineradicable outdoor or even nomadic cast. In weather like ours even the sculpture of Chartres would merge in an indeterminate mass of ornament, and St Theodore and Sainte Modeste become mere decoration instead of being the radiant individuals that they are. That may have been the reason why our sculptors, when they wanted to compel us to notice their handiwork, provided strongly accented erotic focal points of interest.

There can be no doubt that the English weather has fostered a pronounced degree of sensitiveness to nuances and made both men and things more mellow. It lays a sort of patina on them. But the qualities it has generated last only so long as the range of variability in the weather does not exceed the range of tolerance of these peoples of the temperate lands. If they go into hot countries their refinements wear out, and they tend to exhibit the hard core of their personality, turning sour and narrow. It was not for nothing that the Ten Commandments were supposed to be non-existent east of Suez.

After experiencing the English weather I had no difficulty in understanding why Englishmen became so offensive in India, losing their usual kindliness and equability in human relations. Their sense of proportion broke down, the habit of understatement disappeared, and they became extremists with an incredible stridency in their opinions, which became raw and crude. In many cases they degenerated into outright cads, and the more sensitive or specialized the English organism, the more warped it became. I have constructed a scale of the former offensiveness of the English in India by categories. In it I have placed the *mem-sahib* first for unpleasantness to us, with the Anglican clergyman as a close second. This was natural, because the *mem-sahib* was far more delicate than the *sahib*, and the Anglican clergyman was certainly the most specialized Englishman who came to India. The ill-natured peevishness of the women and the uncharitable arrogance of the priests were inconceivable in anyone brought up in the English tradition.

But what could the poor creatures do? If the pride of power and race made them so, the climate and weather of a tropical country did not have a less powerful hand in the transformation. Many of those Englishmen who came to serve in India as officers, civil servants, or clergymen would have been successful and even lovable Wodehouse or Saki heroes at home. But whatever they might have been capable of standing up to there, including dreadful aunts, they could not be expected to stand up to 110° F. without harm. Seven years in India made Kipling incandescent, seventeen would have calcined him. Even as it was, the Indian sojourn made him incapable of loving any Indian with a mind, and led him to reserve all his affection for what could be called the human fauna of the country.

If a moral is to be drawn from all this, it is a simple one. Never demand more from the spirit than the flesh has the power to give, and never, never in any circumstances seek to put asunder those whom God or Nature has joined together, for instance, the Englishman and his weather.

V

MONEY AND THE ENGLISHMAN

INTERESTED AS I WAS in everything English from childhood, I could not possibly have failed to read and hear about their economic conditions and problems. But I gave no attention to them, because I knew I should not be able to understand them. In an age of economics I am not only ignorant of the subject but even contemptuous of it. But economics in its everyday and human form cannot be avoided by anyone, and it happens that in this aspect it has been the concern as much of the moralists as of the economists. Whatever little I shall have to say about the Englishman's relations with money will be said from the moral standpoint.

Now, in the West, or to be more precise in Great Britain and Western Europe, there is nothing more difficult to estimate than a man's exact degree of attachment to money. He will confess to even the most depraved of passions, but not to his love of the thing which makes life in the world possible, a love which within its limits is both reasonable and decent. Here at all events, the moralist has fully succeeded in making hypocrisy a homage paid by vice to virtue. Therefore, if anyone wishes to get an insight into a man's attitude towards money in the West, he has to resort to an indirect line of investigation, to look for symptoms and watch behaviour. But even in the symptoms and behaviour a man will be as wary over money as wild animals are about their young.

So I never asked an Englishman how much love of money he had in his heart, but looked out for symptoms. Naturally, I looked for those which were the easiest to come upon in Hindu society, that is to say, the religious symptoms of the love of money. If I visited the house of an English family I tried quietly to find out if in any part of it there was a private shrine for a god or goddess of money, or for an economic form of their own God. Those Englishmen who would consider this to have been a fantastic thing to do should remember that such a shrine is precisely the thing I cannot escape noticing in every normal Hindu home, even though it may be Westernized up to a certain point. In all these homes there is a little sanctum, unfortunately most tawdrily furnished and decorated in these days, which is devoted to the goddess Lakshmi, who confers prosperity. Of course it goes without saying that I did not find any such shrine in any English home, though in a number of great houses I saw private chapels, which were, however, devoted to normal Christian worship.

In the shops, too, I missed the image of any god who was likely to be a counterpart of our elephant-headed god of success, Ganesa, who presides over all our enterprises, particularly financial ones. Our religiosity covers every aspect of money-making, including the dishonest and violent. There were no more devoted worshippers of the goddess Kali than the Thugs. Christianity does not seem to have been directly involved in financial transactions, and so far as I have read the Anglican liturgy I do not find in it any reference to money-making though there are prayers for protection against natural calamities.

It might be thought that I am drawing a more or less fictitious comparison, and making too much of a state of affairs which was prevalent in the past and is now disappearing in Hindu society. That is not so. Among us the religious approach to economic affairs is as common today as it ever was, though perhaps it should be admitted that in one sense we have become ultra-modern. There is no other country in the world today in which the tribe of pundits called economists are held in greater honour. Perhaps they are the only pundits who are at all honoured by us now. So India has become an El Dorado for every kind of economist from every part of the world. We are engaged in creating a gigantic syncretistic economic cult, in which are to be combined American, English, German, French, Soviet, and Japanese economics, and we are ready, for fear of giving offence to any economic theory about which we have not heard as yet, to erect an altar to the Unknown Economist.

But this has not involved, and on account of its very

catholicity could not involve, any repudiation of the most ancient of our economic cults. Ever since the Rigvedic age we have had economic gods, and we shall continue to have them. Just as we do not even now leave medical treatment solely to the doctor or the surgeon, but requisition the priest and the astrologer, so also we call upon the gods to help us in our economic and technological ventures even in what is described in current economic jargon as the public sector. For instance, when the great dam at Bhakra was formally opened there were Vedic rites to ensure its success. In the personal sphere the economist has no place at all. There, in so far as our own efforts are inadequate, we rely upon the occult powers.

This should be enough to show that I was not setting up a forced contrast between our outlook and that of the English people when I said that I failed to get any clue to their devotion to money from their religious observances. But since I did fail, I tried another approach, and watched their secular behaviour. Here, too, I came up against a barrier of reticence which baffled me. In our society money-making is an open conspiracy, if it is a conspiracy at all. We do not, however, regard it as such. In our eyes it is an occupation which can be avowed with pride by every honest and honourable man. Indeed, as long as we remain in the world we are expected to put money above everything else. The notion of sordidness simply does not exist among us. As a consequence, the process of money-making can be observed as easily in our country as love-making, about which I shall have to say something presently, can be in the West. But in English society there is a good deal of prudery over this. I could not help thinking that it was curious for a people who were described as shopkeepers, and are admitted to be acquisitive and capitalistic, not to discuss the problems and methods of acquisition openly, and to refrain from true shop-talk.

The only thing in their behaviour which seemed to throw an indirect light on the subject was the smoothness with which monetary transactions could be put through. England appeared to be a country of easy money, in the moralist's sense of the term. That is to say, everybody there was not only expected to pay his dues promptly and regularly, but also, generally speaking, did so. In our society the willingness to pay decreases as the capacity to pay increases. What struck me even more forcibly was the readiness of public bodies to part with money, and trust individuals.

I have already said that every nation gets the cats it deserves; so it is with banks, and that was an important discovery. I made it as soon as I presented my first cheque in England. The clerk looked at it, pulled out a drawer, and handed me the money across the counter. I was so astounded by this that I could not help asking, 'But do you not send cheques to the ledger for verifying the signature and balance?' The clerk only smiled in reply, but a lady who was standing by my side said, 'We don't do any such thing in this country.'

Other public bodies seemed to have the same pattern of behaviour. As soon as I arrived in London my friend from the B.B.C. took out some money from his pocket, gave it to me, and said that it was for the expenses of my first few days. Two things in this transaction surprised me: first, that the Accounts Department of the B.B.C. had trusted him with cash, and, secondly, that I was paid the money without any formality. What followed was even more exceptional in my experience of dealing with public departments. I had agreed to write some talks for the B.B.C., and it paid me half the fee, a large sum of money by my standards, in advance. I was also permitted to leave England without any guarantee as to the fulfilment of the contract. I am ashamed to say that I did not reciprocate this treatment by even delivering the scripts within the stipulated time, but took nearly a year to finish them.

In the shops, too, I found a general attitude of unsuspiciousness. At Stratford-upon-Avon I was buying some silver, and finding that I had not enough ready money with me I gave a cheque to the owner of the shop, and requested her to send the articles to my London address when it had been cashed. She gave me the goods then and there. Elsewhere, too, I found no difficulty in paying by cheque, though I have been told that many shops do not accept cheques from unknown customers.

These incidents, small as they were, could not but influence my opinion of the English people. Personally, I was put in a very happy mood to find banks and shops so trustful, and as regards a formal moral judgement I shall say that even if no very high virtues could be attributed to the English people on the strength of these indications, they at least revealed the existence of commercial honesty on a more or less wide scale. The English people seemed to have extended the principle they had put forward in regard to personal and political liberty to their monetary transactions, to say that love of money in order to be enjoyed must be restricted.

But even this belongs to the negative side of the English character, about which I have written, and does not reveal any positive approach to money. My search for this was virtually futile on the earning front, and I could only assume *a priori* that, like all other peoples, they also liked to have money, and as much of it as possible. But as soon as I moved over to the spending front the whole aspect of the search changed. On this side there was as much assertiveness as there was secrecy on the other. Indeed, here they gave their position away.

What I had read about the English people had given me the idea that they had a two-party system in their spending, as they had in their politics. There was the party of the savers, and there was the party of the spenders. Since in English politics the party names originated as terms of abuse and were boastfully taken over by the abused party, I shall follow the precedent and call these two parties the Misers and the Spendthrifts. Like the political parties, or like ritualism and anti-ritualism and High Church and Low Church doctrines, they have alternated in English life from age to age. On the whole, I believe, it is the Spendthrifts who have been longer in power. Here, too, the political analogy holds. I have made a rough calculation that between December 1783, when William Pitt the Younger became Prime Minister, and 1958, the Conservatives or Conservative equivalents have been in power for one hundred and thirteen years, while the Liberals or Liberal equivalents have held it for sixty-two years, giving a ratio of nearly 3 to 2. The periods in which spending has been fashionable and highly regarded in England must bear about the same proportion to the periods in which thrift has been equally respectable.

It is natural to infer from this that spending is the positive urge of the English people, and saving the corrective. Or to put it in slightly different words, spending is the ideal, and frugality the practical correlative of that ideal. With us, on the contrary, hoarding is a pleasure as well as a virtue (a formidable combination), and spending at best a stern duty, but normally a pain. An associated difference between us and the English people is that we cannot, like them, spend money in a planned and deliberate manner, but stand in need of some external pressure or stimulus. For people of moderate means among us, who are of course the majority, this force is the compulsion of living. But for those who have wealth, it is temptation, passion, or panic.

But to come back to what I saw in England. When I was there the Spendthrifts seemed to be in power as decisively as the so-called Tories. If nothing else had indicated that to me, the shops did, in their numbers and splendour — continuous as the stars that shine and twinkle on the Milky Way. If anybody had told me about them before I saw them myself I should have had difficulty in believing him. Not that I had not read about the shops in London and Paris, but actually to go into them was like falling in love after having only read novels.

There was an incredible variety and abundance of goods, and at all prices. For instance, I was specially advised to buy a pair of shoes. In India if I want to buy them I have a choice of only two makes and about four styles acceptable to me. In London and four other towns of England I contemplated hundreds of them, till I lost my faculty for making a selection. So, if in the end I did buy a pair, it was through the help of an obliging shop-assistant in Bond Street. I think I should have gone mad if I had had to decide about clothes, or furniture, or glass, or china.

What really astonished me was the amount of wholly superfluous merchandise on sale even in small towns. Among these I shall only mention two, the flowers and the silver. Flowers, which today are and tomorrow are not and which therefore do not constitute investment, could be bought in cartloads in every part of London. I was told that they were expensive, and expensive they were, but unless there had been people who were willing to pay for them they would not have been stocked. As regards silver, I am fully aware of the connection that exists between the second-hand silver in the shop-windows and taxation, but in similar circumstances the metal would have been melted down in my country, and not been allowed to retain its useless art forms. I made two token purchases of both just to show my loyalty to the cult of superfluous expenditure.

Now about food. What silly things had I not been told about its being both scarce and monotonous! After seeing things for myself I wrote to my family, and that too very soon after my arrival, not to have any fears on that score. If for nothing else I should have been grateful for the simple fact that I was having good cows' milk for the first time in about twenty years, in London of all places, after coming from a cow-worshipping country. But I was not wholly a baby in matters of food, so I had other things as well. Indeed, I could lunch or dine on anything I liked. The very first thing that I had in London was a Camembert, which I had been wanting to taste for years. I related my gastronomical adventures in detail to my family, and here is an extract from one of my letters:

'One of the highlights of the day [on which I also met Bertrand Russell] was the lunch. The restaurant cooks sole in thirty-two different ways, and I had one kind which was cooked in white wine, with shrimps, oysters, mussels and mushrooms. For hors-d'oeuvres we had smoked salmon, which was amazingly good, and as dessert I had such pineapple as I had not eaten since I left East Bengal nearly thirty years ago, and we washed it all down with a fine bottle of Chablis, which cost more than my Château-Yquem at home.' (I hope the sordid reference will be forgiven, it was a private letter in which I wanted to show my gratitude to my hosts.)

People in my country tell me that this was exceptional. Of course it was. When one speaks of French gastronomy one does not have the everyday food of the French in mind. The question was whether anyone wanting it could have good living in England. I found that I could. All this must sound absurd to English good-livers, but I have to convince my people who have come to believe from what they have heard from those who have lived in England that the English eat only potato chips and cabbage.

There were not only a large number of shops, there also seemed to be a hierarchy and even caste system among them, which in its own way threw some light on the English people's philosophy of spending. When I told a young lady at Cambridge that I had seen some good shops in a certain street in London she observed that there were some frightfully cheap ones at the upper end. Cambridge, she explained, was different from London in this respect. In London there were very expensive as well as very cheap shops, but Cambridge was not extreme in either direction, and yet was very good in the middle ranges, with, however, sufficient elbow room within that range.

I think it is this kind of attitude to shops which has led the Bond Street Association to adopt and display a rather attractive slogan in their windows: 'It costs you no more to buy, but it means so much more to you.' I have, however, been told recently that middle-class people in England feel shy of going into Bond Street shops on account of their clothes, which they fear are not smart enough for the shop-assistants, who will therefore look down their noses at them. I had no idea that in order to shop in Bond Street one had to be tailored in Savile Row, and so I walked into the shops in the most nondescript of clothes. I suppose the fact of my being a dark-skinned foreigner condoned my inadequacy.

But if what I have heard is true, I would say that the owners of the Bond Street shops should do something about it. They should not allow the effect of their nice slogan as an invitation to spend in Bond Street to be whittled down by the manners of their assistants. I should certainly hesitate in the future to enter a Bond Street shop.

I can hardly say how it gladdened the heart of a spendthrift in both principle and, so far as my means have permitted, in practice, to find myself in a country in which spending was respectable. I liked the English people for their devotion to spending — 'That's the way the money goes.'

Of course, I also know that their Government and economists have black looks for them on account of this, and are doing their best to wean them from the habit. It is quite possible that the Government and the economists are right in their way, they know their business; but I am sure that they do not know the psychology of their people. They are also inconsistent. They cannot go on boasting about the so-called Welfare State in the way they do, and yet do things which deprive this Welfare State of all meaning. Does the Welfare State stand for meanness for the sake of maintaining the balance of payments, or does it constitute an opportunity for realizing one of the most deep-seated ambitions of the English people?

I do not call it the desire for a high standard of living, which is a shabby economists' catchword. The English people have always desired a much more generous thing — style in living. To live in style and be careless about money has in the past been the privilege of the English upper classes. So even those who could not afford to be careless have pretended to be so. At last, with the coming of the Welfare State the opportunity for living like their betters has come to the English people at large. If they are going to be prevented from doing so, they are bound to feel sore. I will say that in that event their victory over poverty will be too much like their victory in two World Wars. I hope the English people will resist the insidious degradation. In any case, they have taught me that the best use for money is to spend it on the good things of life.

VI

LOVE'S PHILOSOPHY

IF THE ENGLISH PEOPLE'S dealings with money came as something like a discovery to me, there was another thing which I might call a revelation, though its evidence was scattered on the surface of their existence. It was their attitude towards love. In England, as indeed all over Europe, love seemed to be a primary motivation of human beings, a major occupation of men and women, and as serious a pursuit as money-making is in our society. Yet nobody seemed to be conscious that here was a special feature of Western life of which one had to take immediate notice, and I am sure if I had told them so they would have been surprised. In regard to love, Hindu society and Western society stand at opposite poles, and although this fact was not wholly unsuspected by me, the radical nature of the difference was a thing totally unexpected.

To a man like me, who is never able to separate life from literature, another difference seemed hardly less striking. In England it did not take me long to find out that love within its manifold expressions but fundamental unity, which I had met with in English literature, was not primarily a literary phenomenon. This statement would appear to be very odd unless it is remembered that I am a Hindu, and that in our society it is very difficult to observe the workings of love in human beings, and to watch love-making at first hand is virtually impossible. However, the history of love in Bengali Hindu society is fairly well established. It was introduced from the West much later than tobacco or potatoes, but has neither been acclimatized as successfully, nor has taken as deep roots, as these two plants.

We in Bengal began to deal with love from the literary end. That is to say, at first it was transferred to Bengali literature from

English literature, and then taken over from literature to life. As a result of this double transplantation, the plant remains delicate, and a hothouse atmosphere is needed for its survival. I think what is true of Bengal is also true of Hindu society as a whole. It has never needed love for marriage, family, and similar social institutions. Even now we speak of two kinds of marriage, marriage properly so called, legitimate marriage so to speak, and 'love-marriage'. The mention of the latter always raises a smile, and the usual reaction of a Bengali mother, on hearing of the proposed or clandestinely accomplished 'love-marriage' of a son, is acute palpitation of the heart and high blood-pressure; the father's is not clinical, but it is sterner, and is concerned with the method, which constitutes a defiance of *patria potestas*.

Certainly, in many marriages love comes, but it is *ex post facto*, and also transient — it burns with a short-lived lambency on married life, like cognac on a pudding already made with other ingredients. It is a marginal luxury, a fancy value, which is never taken into explicit account as one of the pleasures of the married state. Altogether, the Hindu theory and practice foster a certain detachment in respect of love, although in recent times on account of the play of Western influences a number of overtones and undertones have been added, for instance, a strange gladness when wafts of love are borne in on chance winds, or a vague heartache when, thanks to the constant reading of English novels and fiction in the Indian languages modelled on the English and lately to the growing habit of seeing films, the absence of love is felt in life. The popularity of fiction and films in India has a good deal to do with the fact that they are compensatory to actual life. On the whole, however, we can be very happy without love, and indeed not a few of us would consider love well lost for the world.

Therefore when I saw in Western society that love had an independent existence and was not a transference from literature, that was bound to impress me deeply. I also saw that love-making was an easily observable activity. In fact, it was going on everywhere and at all times. I have seen young people falling on one another, crying, and kissing on a studded pedestrian crossing in a wide Paris thoroughfare, thundering with motor traffic. In Rome I spent the last hours of my stay in Europe on the Capitol, and I shall never forget the experience. Though exalted in spirit, I was tired in body, but all the benches were occupied by lovers, and not one couple would make room for an aged and footsore stranger, although to all appearance they had one another to prop themselves up on and hardly needed any additional material support. They were giving a demonstration of love among the ruins.

I saw the same spectacle in England, even in the Cambridge Backs, almost under the shadow of King's College Chapel. The exhibition is more self-abandoned by the Seine than by the Thames, but the practical result is about equal by the standards of each nation: it makes Englishmen forget their dignity and Frenchmen their intelligence. But the French authorities, conscious of the awful consequence of a failure of intelligence on the part of Frenchmen, have put up the following notice on all the bridges: *Secours! En cas de noyade, ou accident, demandez la brigade fluviale ou les sapeurs-pompiers.* In England, however, the tradition of individual freedom is too strong for even such a discreet attempt at safeguarding English dignity. So everybody is allowed to forget that the only places where love-making does not look somewhat ridiculous are, first, the stage, where it is meant to be seen but not felt, and, next, a private place in which it is meant to be felt but not seen.

It must not be assumed, however, that everybody in England is unruffled by this over-demonstrative behaviour. When I spoke about it to the wife of an English friend of mine, she asked me indignantly if I was not going to write about it. I replied that perhaps it was too namby-pamby a thing to write about. Her husband immediately observed that this was precisely what he could not convince his wife about. She was sure that these goings-on could not be innocent. But the husband added that these people were always like that, and there was nothing in it at all, they would spoon by the hour without coming to much harm. Though my knowledge was very superficial, I was inclined to agree with him, because I thought there were some kinds of foolishness which could not be vicious.

I am, for all that, writing about the subject. Nevertheless, it should not be thought that I am assuming superior airs. It is possible to miss the real significance of the phenomenon by doing so, for this love-making runs fairly deep though it is not of the still sort. It certainly is not a recent fashion, or a result of the laxer standards in matters of sex, about which one is always reading. Love-making as a widespread, popular, semi-popular, and aristocratic activity has always been present in Western society. It has been going on in country lanes and cottages, great houses and parks, for ages, and no one who has read English literature can remain unaware of the fact.

Today's obtrusive love-making, which appears so trivial, is really a democratic and therefore cheapened and vulgarized form of one of the most significant movements in the evolution of sensibility, which has brought about the emergence of romantic and idealized love as a basis of the intimate relationship between men and women. It is Europe's special contribution to the life of passion of mankind.

Even this is not all. In the West love-making is as much social as biological. They have made family life dependent on love, and so long as their family life remains they will not be able to break this affiliation, so that even if love were to go on asserting its independence in the manner it is doing today, half of it will remain under the power of the family. The affiliation is best illustrated in Jane Austen. Some people have criticized her for making husband-hunting a barefaced motive in her heroines. But she was too great a moralist and at the same time too fine a realist to be able to forget the social matrix of love. Still she did not make love *qua* love less intense than it is in, say, Emily and Charlotte Brontë, although her treatment of it was miniaturesque.

All peoples of Aryan origin realized very early in their evolution that the relationship of the sexes had to be lifted out of its biological foundations, if it was to give any lasting happiness. So the Hindus no less than the Christians made marriage a sacrament, and finding that this was not enough, brought in additional values. Here, however, the ways of Hindus and Europeans parted. In Europe, throughout the Middle Ages, love was idealized and romanticized by chivalry and *courtoisie*, the songs of the troubadours, and the vows of the knights. Mediaeval love, even when made utterly fanciful, did not lose nobility. Conceits like valentines made it more charming rather than less, and in Dante it became something which hardly touched the earth. When, in later ages, the peoples of Europe widened its idea still further, they never went backwards to identify it with the physical impulse, and modern Occidentals must not think that their obsession with sex and their boasted realism in regard to it are very up-to-date. We Hindus, who have had time to become more or less *blasé* about it, cannot help regarding it with a certain degree of tired and impatient boredom.

It is interesting to see that in Europe love was transformed in such a manner that even what was regarded as the wrong kind of love evoked more pity than repulsion. One has only to compare the associations of such names as Messalina and Francesca, or set the amours of Napoleon's sister Pauline against the love affairs of her contemporary Mme de Staël, or read the two extraordinary stories of the Châtelaine of Vergi and Manon Lescaut, or for that matter, Anna Karenina, to feel the difference.

We Hindus on the other hand left love to take care of itself in the best manner it could, and took our stand on the idea of fidelity. In Europe the idealization of relations of the sexes was the work of the man; in India or, to be more accurate, in Hindu society, it was that of the woman. If anybody tells you that the Hindu ideal of wifely devotion is an imposition by a patriarchal society, a tyranny prompted by male jealousy, do not believe a word of it. It simply is not true. With us, paradoxical as it may sound, it was the women who stole the wind out of the sails of the men. They set up an ideal of faithfulness which not only made the noose and the sack unnecessary, but even the worth of the man of no consequence. Hindu women gloried in the idea of *sati* (which is not the same thing as the *suttee* of the English language, though the word is the same), and gave their love irrespective of the merits of the recipient, in which their defiant love partook of the quality of God's love in Christianity, which is given freely without any reference to the worth of man. We are often told by our Western friends that they just cannot understand our system of marriage. Most of us do not understand theirs either. In any case, countless millions have found happiness in our system, and it is not to be spoken of lightly.

But, of course, neither the one nor the other is without its shortcomings. The greatest failure of the Western attitude is that in making love an end in itself it is encouraging love to be a wild thing, which sends men and women out on a selfish chase after a will-o'-the-wisp. At times, it prompts cruelties which far surpass any that the R.S.P.C.A. deals with, and which are inexplicable in an age in which, in the collective social life of man, compassion has in some respects become a malady. Let me tell an anecdote in this connection.

One evening my wife and I were dining with an English couple. It was a very intimate, candle-lit party, and the talk turned on love. I held forth about what I considered to be the only sane attitude towards it, which was not the Hindu view, though it was opposed to the Western. It was more or less personal. I admitted that love was something quite precious in the lives of men and women and if it came we had every right to feel blessed. But there were so many other things in life which were no less needed for human happiness, which we could not command, had to go without, and were even perfectly reconciled to going without. Therefore, if we did not have love, that was no justification for throwing ourselves into a tragic pose, and least of all for inflicting unhappiness and misery on others.

At the end of my lecture, our hostess got up, placed one hand on the shoulder of her husband and slightly leaned her head on the other shoulder, and said, 'About this love, of which you think so ill, I'll only say that but for the love I bear towards my husband I should not be what I am.'

She was a straightforward English girl without any intellectual, aesthetic, or emotional pretensions, but as she spoke such a light came into her eyes and such a music in her voice that I was momentarily taken aback, and considered if I was not speaking about things of which I knew nothing, as a person who has not known motherhood might speak about it.

I have subsequently heard that they are now divorced. I simply do not and cannot understand this. I ask myself, 'Are these men and women so much in love with love that they have ceased to take pity on human beings?' After all, it is one of their moralists who has said that 'it is one of the noblest qualities of our nature that we are able so easily to dispense with greater perfection.'

The Hindu concept on its part does not always bring about any idealization of love and allows sex relations to remain at the bodily level, fostering sensuality in wedlock. It also puts too great a burden on the woman.

So, considering everything, one might say that, although the Westerners have made their choice and we ours, the resultant satisfaction and dissatisfaction balance each other, and we are no worse off than they are, and they no worse than we, which made me give the following title to the article which I wrote on the subject and published in one of our newspapers:

Life plus *Love* = *Life* minus *Love*

That, I think, was a fair equation, and no provocation given by silliness in the West or injustice in the East will make me give up this view.

I know I have been rather orthodox over this subject, and this was very quickly detected by a very famous Englishman with whom I once had a conversation. He had listened to my political views, and commented, `You are very unorthodox.' Then the talk drifted to the relations of men and women. He listened to my exposition of the Hindu view, and as he did so I thought I saw the faint suggestion of a smile at the corners of his mouth. When I concluded, he said abruptly with a twinkle in his eyes, `You are very orthodox.' I could only reply, `I am not a bad sort at bottom, though I have to criticize my people for their good.'

VII

JOHN BULL, LOST AND FOUND

I HAVE SET DOWN a few of my impressions of the positive as well as the negative attitudes of the English people, and shall now conclude this account of their manners with some general observations. The most widely advertised conception of the Englishman that the outside world used to have till recently was that of John Bull, who was, however, different things to different nations. In India he was identified with the sojourning English type, the Anglo-Indian of olden days. These Englishmen as a rule treated us with authoritarian solicitude mixed with a certain amount of condescension, but sometimes also with icy snobbishness, and occasionally even with loud and berserker bad temper.

Certain classes in Indian society were always discussing their behaviour, but self-respecting Indians normally kept away from them, or maintained only formal official relations. Our great poet Tagore, who shunned them, as indeed he could be expected to do, felt exasperated when he was compelled to meet them. Of one such meeting he wrote: 'In general I cannot stand the Anglo-Indians, and at the dinner last night I saw another example of their outrageous behaviour. The principal of the college here is an *outré* Englishman, with a long nose, cunning eyes, a yard of chin, clean shaven cheeks, deep voice, and a drawling articulation without *r*'s, altogether a full-blown John Bull. He was running down our people ....I can hardly tell you how I felt.... Just think how they see us, these people who come to the table of a Bengali, and cannot keep themselves from speaking about us as this man did.'

Would Englishmen today recognize one of themselves or even the traditional John Bull in this picture? Most probably this

Englishman was from Oxford or Cambridge. Yet men of this type must have existed. Englishmen who had lived in India were noticed even in England when they returned there on retirement. In the eighteenth century they were called Nabobs, and later simply Anglo-Indians. They were a distinct set. A friend of mine who was in England in the early 'twenties told me the following story. He was sitting in a very crowded bus when a lady came in. As nobody else got up he did not do so either. Upon that an Englishman who had come in just after the lady began to abuse him, saying that Indians did not know any manners. The Indian said that even the countrymen of the lady had not offered their seats, and the other Englishmen supported him. When this friend of mine reached the house where he was going, he found the same imperious Englishman also coming in. The lady whom he had come to see asked him if he knew the gentleman who had just gone up, for he had been in India. He was a famous former Lieutenant-Governor of an Indian province. Perhaps I may cite Tagore again on this subject. He had been invited one evening to sing in the house of a lady whom he had known in India and who lived outside London, but was sent back without being given dinner. When he related this adventure to a girl of the family with which he lived she laughed and said, 'You must not think that *we* are like that, it is the style of hospitality brought over from *your* country.'

Now with the exception of two missionaries and my old chief in the News Division of All India Radio, who was an Englishman, I had never come in close contact with English people till about five or six years ago. So I have no personal testimony to offer about their behaviour or misbehaviour. But I had heard enough to have become curious to see whether the type was to be found in England today, and I remained watchful.

I did meet some Englishmen who had once worked and lived in India, some of them in very high official positions. But unless I had been told about their antecedents I should not have thought from anything in their manners or appearance that they had been in India. Yet some of those whom I met were controversial and unpopular figures in India. After meeting one of them I wrote to my family: 'Mr S——is quite different from what I thought he would be. He does not have any suggestion of being an Anglo-Indian (old sense) in his talk and manners.

His rooms are beautiful, and there are some fine English ivory miniatures of his ancestors and ancestresses.'

So far as I could see, there was not only no rancour on account of the loss of India, there was not even any hangover of the psychological tension to which I have already referred, and which life in India generated in Englishmen. Their proper environment seemed to have reclaimed them, and restored their natural self. I might use a musical term and say that it had effaced the accidentals and re-established the normal key.

Not to speak of the *ci-devants* or the *émigrés*, I did not even see the traditional John Bull, stout, overbearing, and contemptuous of foreigners, who at one time was the object both of insular pride and Continental mirth. One incident among my experiences could, if an uncharitable interpretation were put on it, be regarded as pointing to his survival, but even at its worst it was evidence only for the existence of a little John Calf, and nothing more.

As I was coming out of Canterbury Cathedral I observed a little English boy of about six sitting on the grass and looking at me with an intense gaze, like a lion cub watching a distant zebra. When I came near him he began to rise slowly on his knees, and while still half kneeling raised his arm, pointed a finger at me, and cried out in his sharp treble, 'You're from Africa!' This was the moment for me to scream 'Colour prejudice!' and send a bitter letter to one of our newspapers, for there is nothing a Hindu resents more than being taken for a negro by a white man. But I shouted back, 'No, from India!' The body dropped on the grass and kept his eyes fixed on it. I thought he had been abashed, but when I met him in another part of the close the mischievous little fellow again piped out, 'You're from Africa!' He clearly felt that he had succeeded in teasing me.

But if this incident called for any revenge it was taken more than amply for me by a French workman in Paris. I was sitting at the foot of one of the flights of steps which lead from the upper to the lower quays of the Seine, on the left bank and opposite the apse of Notre-Dame. I have always considered this aspect of the cathedral with its flying buttresses showing over the clumps of trees to be the finest view of it. As I sat looking at it, a clock housed in a small gable in the roof of the south transept struck an hour. I pulled out my watch to compare, and suddenly I heard a voice above me say, 'Neuf heures.' Not quite catching the words, I looked up and saw a French workman perched half-way up the steps. He spread out both his hands, folded one thumb and showed the rest of the fingers to me to explain what he had said. Then he asked, 'Monsieur est anglais?' I was taken aback by his idea of the size and looks of an Englishman, and replied, 'Mais non, indien.' 'Ah oui, indien!' he replied and showed such readiness to open a conversation that I, having fears for my spoken French, ran away, still wondering how he could have said what he had said.

Of the notorious stand-offishness of Englishmen I saw nothing. I recall with gratitude the opportunities I had for seeing their home life and also the invitations I could not accept on account of my overcrowded sightseeing programme. I must have been a very unfamiliar character to them, yet they treated me like one of themselves. 'Come and see how we live,' they would say, and take me round their bedrooms, nurseries, kitchens, cellars and attics. In a friend's house I inquired about the fuel they used. It was in the country, and I was told that they had anthracite in an Aga cooker. I had been hearing about the Aga for twenty years, and was very eager to see it. I was taken to the kitchen.

I spent one afternoon in the house of a friend on the outskirts of London. The husband and wife had created a beautiful little garden at the back of their house, and remembering the tradition of lawn-keeping in England they apologized for a hand's-breadth of yellow in the grass. After I had come back to India my friend sent me photographs of the garden, and wrote: 'Everyone was pleased to have met you, especially as you fell in with all our habits and customs as if you had lived among us for years.' This was a very handsome compliment, and a no less handsome one was paid to me by a lady, for she took me to her house when it was being painted.

One of my last evenings was spent at the house of another friend. He and his wife made me feel so much at home that I could not have felt more so even in my own house. I let myself go with gusto, and was ready to go on indefinitely, when my hostess got up and said, 'Mr Chaudhuri, you must go now, for you have to go to Winchester early in the morning.' I was to catch my train at seven. I jumped up and replied, 'I must obey you, Mrs P—, you are *in loco uxoris* for me here.' The husband laughed. But they were not trying to get rid of me. They drove me back to Bloomsbury from near Hampton Court, and went back only after setting me down at the door of my hotel.

I have still to speak about the very last evening, spent at a friend's flat in Kensington. Hearing of my interest in wines he brought out a bottle of *vin rouge*, over which we chatted until it was nearly midnight. I was to go to the airport at ten, and had not only to finish my packing but also to write a sheaf of letters. When I got up at five next morning to face my tasks I had no tired feeling. That was not due to the wine; nothing makes social life more tiring than lack of intimacy.

In spite of all this there is no doubt that old John Bull is still alive for a very large number of my countrymen in England, who are there for education, business, or other purposes. Even after staying there for a relatively long time most of them remain without English friends. They live a lonely and at times very unhappy life, grumbling about everything from food to social customs. They have friends only among their countrymen, and feel that the English are a proud, cold, and even snobbish people. Many of them develop into a type which is complementary to the old Anglo-Indian, living in a country and yet nursing a grievance against it. Not a few turn rabidly anti-English.

I had heard about this, and learned something from first-hand experience. I was even asked by some thoughtful young countrymen of mine to say something about this attitude, with the object of persuading them to give it up, to a group of students at Oxford. I could not do so, but I certainly should have liked to if I had had the time.

I can see what it is due to, and one of the reasons is that most of my countrymen go to England, not out of love for things English, but only for vocational advantages. The dominant class in India is very paradoxical in one thing: it will never give any well-paid job to anyone who has not been educated or trained in the West, and yet it will not teach the men whom it compels to go abroad to love or respect anything outside the country. Therefore their enforced stay irks them.

But it is no less due to the fact that English social life is still English social life, and trying to enter it is like entering a club.

Physical nearness means very little there. In my London hotel, which was not large, I did not notice anyone making friends with the other inmates. An African, obviously a highly educated man, always took his meals alone, and even *I* did not go up and talk to him, falling in, I suppose, with the spirit of the society. On my part, I too did not make any friends in any of the hotels I stayed in, and hardly even talked to the other residents. The only person in England who opened a conversation with me was an Irishman in a railway carriage. All Indians, and I believe Americans and Continentals too, get a poor impression of the Englishman's sociability.

Social intercourse in England, as everybody knows, has to pass through 'proper channels', and it is not as easy to be rightly canalized in it as for one's aeroplane at an airport. This applies not only to foreigners in England but to the natives as well. Yet perhaps for us Indians this is not the greatest difficulty, which arises from the fact that we cannot cash in on the introductions fully, because we and Englishmen belong to different psychological species, which are not a bit less real than zoological species. The English animal will not take the initiative to make friends with the exotic creature, and so even though we are of the guest team we have to do the honours. I shall quote my son once again. He is no believer in intimate personal relations between Englishmen and Indians, but has succeeded in solving the problem to a certain point. He has written to us:

> 'The English well-bred middle-class type is so very English that it is impossible to get to know their various little ways unless you have lived with them. They will relax only in the privacy of their homes. They are too polite and considerate to think of imposing their habits on foreigners, yet they get upset if people do not conform to English ways in England, a marvellous specimen of human beings, very complex altogether. Living among them I realize why I get on with the English people if they themselves respond.'

So for most of us, old John Bull survives in English social life. To my thinking, he also does in the international relations of the English people, which will sound unconvincing unless it is remembered that John Bull, like Janus, always had two faces, the conservative and the radical. The conservative John Bull was symbolized in world affairs by men like Palmerston, but better still by actions like the bombardment of Alexandria. This John Bull is dead, or is to be found only in a very refined, or alternatively secret form, and even in this avatar he is rejected by more than half of his people.

But there was also another John Bull who had a remarkable flair for falling headlong in love with anybody he considered oppressed or unfairly treated, and who, provided he had got hold of what he regarded as a moral principle, never hesitated to go the whole hog in its pursuit, however shoddy or sloppy it might be. In its light he would haul his own people over the coals, applaud every enemy of England, and provide ample ammunition for attacking his own country. Very few people seem to know that three-quarters of the arguments of Indian nationalism, as distinct from its subconscious urges, was the pure milk of the radical John-Bullite word, and bore the label 'Made in England'. This John Bull is still going strong.

But if I think that John Bull lives on, I have something else too in mind, and that is John Bull, not in his relations with foreign peoples and the outside world, but John at home in his private capacity, as an English personality. There is no doubt that he exists, although in his case the distinction that English law makes between the innate dangerousness of a bull and of a cow is almost wholly obsolete. If anyone falls foul of him now and is gored he will have to prove that the animal was dangerous.

To me it seemed that the John Bull reformed and redivivus could be most easily recognized among the English working people, a manly and shrewd set of men, who were always friendly but never impertinent, who knew their place and yet were not servile, and who wanted not only to live but also to understand things in their own way. If any vulgarity has lately appeared among these descendants of the men who fought at Crecy and Agincourt, it is not in the stock, it has come and is coming from that modern thing, universal primary education.

Even this working-class John Bull is sometimes misunderstood by us. I remember a story which a friend of mine, a Bengali, told me in the early 'thirties. He was passing through London on his way back to India after living for some years in the United States, and was getting his shoes blacked somewhere in the City. The man looked up at him as he polished, and asked, 'What country are you from, sir?' When he was told that it was India, he brightened up and asked again, 'What do you think of our rule there?' 'That is what they are like, those English,' commented my friend indignantly, 'even their shoe-blacks think that they are our masters.' To me both the question and the reaction to it seemed so typical that I laughed out loud, but the attempts that I made to persuade my friend to take a less lurid view of the matter failed completely.

However, I saw very little of the English working classes, and when an English friend in India heard that, he observed that I had not seen the English people at all. This friend may have been a Labourite in his politics, but he was partly right. I did not, however, get the opportunity to meet the working people in the first instance, and then if I had got it I do not think I would have made proper use of it. To go out to study the English workers, between whom and me flowed a wide river of class-consciousness, would have been too much like social research or visiting for my taste. So I kept myself to the class broadly resembling mine. In it, too, I thought I was meeting John Bull with his characteristic outlooks and behaviour. I found that the sophisticated English upper middle-class, inaccessible as it was to us in many respects, was yet much more simple and elemental over the fundamentals of life than we Hindus. Men and women of this class were not quite as specialized as human beings as we were.

Even those two duennas of English life at its highest level, Oxford and Cambridge, formidable as they are as finishing governesses, have not done much to attenuate this simplicity, if indeed that was ever their object. A self-conscious Oxford or Cambridge man can be unattractive in spite of a studied gentleness. But the great majority are not self-conscious in an unpleasant way, though they remain conscious that they have passed through these places. No one who has profited from an Oxford or Cambridge education flaunts his *cachet*, valued as it is in English society. Most of them are like the lawns of their colleges, which do not know what centuries of mowing and rolling have done for them. Others only remember with gratitude what they owe to Oxford and Cambridge. I have always thought it somewhat curious that Englishmen who are always glorifying their public schools, colleges, and universities, never pay any formal tribute of gratitude to their parents. I have not read any acknowledgement of the debt owed to parents and relations written by an Englishman in the manner of the Emperor Marcus Aurelius.

Yet it seems, in the end, it is their parents who teach them at school and college, though at one remove. It is they who have made the schools and universities in their own image, and they feel sure that in these places their sons will be made in the very same image, without their having to take the trouble of licking the adolescent bear-cubs into shape themselves. Thus even higher education in England results ultimately in the perpetuation of the traits of John Bull. In one way, I would say, Oxford and Cambridge men are the most typical John Bulls I have met.

I should, however, illustrate the point I have made about the relative simplicity of the upper middle-class Englishman, or what might be described even as 'under-development' by our standards. This can be done, for one thing, by referring back to their attitude to money. As I have said something about the subject I shall only explain why I consider it to be less *evolved* than ours.

Everybody knows that the human intellect originated as a means of bringing about adjustments of the organism with its material environment. But in the West it has now acquired a life which is largely independent of its purely utilitarian purpose, and man the maker has also become man the thinker, who is honoured as such. On the same analogy, money-making, which in its practical aspect is only a means of living a comfortable life, should have developed into a more or less absolute pursuit, and the money-maker become as much an object of national pride as a great scientist or philosopher. This has happened among us Hindus, but not in the West, where money is still tied to its uses, and the money-maker does not become respectable until he has begun to spend his gains for other ends besides more money-making, and even for bribing intellectuals and philanthropists by creating endowments for their hobbies. Those Occidentals who call us economically backward, or euphemistically 'under-developed', in the pride of technological progress, have no inkling that in another aspect of economic life they are far less developed than we Hindus, who look upon the millionaire as the natural complement of the Sadhu.

The English middle-class is also simple in its attitude to manual work, which has made the servantless household possible. Economic conditions and social changes may have made their contribution to this, but when one remembers to what extent the standard of life of the English upper middle-class depended on a large staff of servants, one realizes that the servantless house would not have worked without a perceptible decline in elegance, comfort, and cleanliness without this pre-existent attitude to bodily labour even in Englishmen of the highest classes.

In our society an official of middle-class origins not only does not carry his briefcase, he does not even take a paper to a colleague, he rings for the peon. This peon on his part will carry papers and files but not packages. When I was working in a Government office in Delhi, a peon was asked one day to bring a bound volume of newspapers, and he refused. On a complaint being made to the Administrative Officer, the latter gave the decision that a peon should not have been expected to carry a load, for which a coolie should have been requisitioned. This same peon will not dust a table, for which another functionary is employed, and the table-duster will not sweep the floor, that being the task of yet another functionary. In our society every rise in status is accompanied by a progressive diminution of physical labour. So when in England I saw shop-assistants sweeping the floor of the shop and even the pavement, and my friends carrying my suitcase for me, I was bound to notice the difference.

There is something monastic in the English attitude to physical labour, but it must not be forgotten that this monastic attitude was itself Western and not brought over from the East with the institution of monasticism. It is no less remarkable that the physical labour of the monks was wholly utilitarian. When we Hindus thought of physical exertion as a means of spiritual catharsis, we indulged in Yoga. Of course, in England, too, physical exercise has been ritualized in the form of games and sport, and perhaps most so in the centres of intellectual training. It might even be said that to a certain extent the ideal of *mens sana in corpore sano* has been put into practice as the reality of inane minds in a tough body. But even at its worst the ritualistic physical culture has remained physical, and has not been resorted to as a means of overriding the laws of nature, including gravitation. But as a general rule, even those Englishmen who make a fetish of ritualized physical exercise remain capable of workaday and useful physical exertion.

But even more strikingly than in these things, the simplicity of the English middle-class appeared to me to be illustrated in their manner of following a profession or career. In our society a man does not mind sacrificing the general business of living for the one or the other. I have seen lawyers devoting themselves to their cases from morning till bedtime, doctors doing the same thing, officials shutting themselves up at home to study their files. And most of them would be thoroughly unhappy if they were not allowed to do so. General conversation in company is not only an unlearned art for them, it is a dissipation in their eyes.

Leisure is a torture to them, and some condemn it. In my early life when I was a clerk, a high official once told me that Calcutta was possibly the worst place to have an office in. I was naturally surprised and asked him why he thought so. He replied, 'It is a big city with many distractions, and nobody cares to come to the office on Sundays. At Ranchi we had nothing to do at home, and nothing to see in the town, and so all of us went to our offices on Sundays.' I sometimes ask them the meaning of all this, and they all plead the compulsion of bread-earning, which is not true, for, to speak only of those who are in Government service, they beg in the most abject manner for extensions of service beyond the age limit even when they have earned a full pension and saved enough to be independent. Still, admitting their plea, I put a Socratic question to them: 'That is perfectly true so far as it goes, but will you tell me why you go on earning a livelihood, sacrificing everything else to it, when you do not *live* at all?' They simply do not understand me.

Taking the attitude to work to the next higher stage, I found the English middle-class to differ from us even more radically. It seemed to me that in selecting a career they took their main interest in life into account, and this interest not only governed the choice but also took the question of money and worldly position–in its stride. Englishmen, if they have a sense of vocation at all, are ready to leave even a well-paid and secure job when they find it coming in the way of what they want to do in life, maybe felt not at all as a mission or grand passion, but only as a matter of simple personal inclination. 'What do you want to do in life?' is a pointless question to most of us. We are ready to do anything provided it gives us wealth, security, worldly position, and power, which mingle as inducements in differing proportions with different persons.

Therefore we also plan our careers in terms of wealth, position, and power, and pursue the selected career with an almost Napoleonic deliberation. We have no indissoluble emotional or ethical ties with anything we are doing at a particular time of our life. If a little more money or prestige is going in another post we do not hesitate to leave the one we are holding for one in a completely different line. The rush of the intellectuals from the universities to the secretariat is one of the most striking career-drifts seen in our country.

All this would appear to Englishmen as being something like an adventurer's outlook on life. But the word *adventurer* is not familiar to us, it would, even when known, be taken as the equivalent of an adventurous person. What, however, is more to the point is the fact that a man who has eliminated all other interests in life in order to follow a profession or a career is a much more specialized being than one who has not. Whether he is regarded by some as an adventurer, *arriviste,* or egoist will not make any difference to that indisputable fact. That brings me back to the point I was wanting to make, that the English middle-class is much more simple and general than we are.

PART III

CULTURAL LIFE

I

SHAKESPEARE IN TODAY'S ENGLAND

I HAVE GIVEN THE title 'Cultural Life' to this section of my account, but I am far from being happy about it. It is likely to give rise to dissatisfaction on all sides. The things I am going to speak about are regarded by the English people as their amusements, and they may feel that I am spoiling their enjoyment by bringing in the pretentious notion of culture. On the other hand, most of my countrymen will miss in them that high purpose which alone can, in their view, justify anybody's describing them as cultural. Therefore, in order to avoid giving offence to any party, if not to succeed in pleasing both, I shall begin with a safe topic, which is amusement in England but culture in India.

It is Shakespeare. We in Bengal used to worship him, and I am one of the last surviving Bengalis who were brought up in that cult. So I found nothing unusual in the celebrations which I saw at Stratford-upon-Avon on the 39Ist anniversary of the poet's birthday. Their formal part: the speeches, the procession, unfurling of the flags, visit to the birth-place, laying of wreaths and posies on the tomb—all this we might have managed more or less in the same way if we had to pay homage to a national hero. Of course, here too I noticed local touches. The speeches were in the form of toasts, and to ram them down we had the following luncheon:

Menu
Melon Rafraîchi
ou
Consommé en gelée
*

Saumon froid, sauce mayonnaise
Pointes d'asperges
ou
Dindonneau et jambon froids
Salade de saison
Pommes nouvelles
*

Gâteau glacé Shakespeare
*

Fromages
*

Café

—and to wash them down we were given a two-page wine list, which for the honour of Stratford was qualified as the '*Abridged* Wine List'. Also, the speeches were made by people who could be expected to know something about the poet and be cogent, and not by politicians or civil servants who thought that they were conferring an honour on Shakespeare or at the most recommending his name for the Honours List.

But everything besides this function in Shakespeare's relations with contemporary England was novel to me. At the very outset I was surprised by the tribute to him that was in.plicit in the apparent prosperity of Stratford. Here was a little town doing quite well on Shakespeare, as the country town in which I was born did on litigation, which in its turn was kept going by the money brought in by jute. I was told elsewhere in England that Shakespeare was dreadfully commercialized at Stratford. It was, however, this very commercialization which gave me the greatest pleasure. As I wrote to my family:

'Stratford is a small town, smaller than Kishorganj of my boyhood. But it has all kinds of old and modern china, antiques, old and modern silver, furniture, and books. Of course, Stratford flourishes on Shakespeare, and even Englishmen say everything at Stratford is commercialized. But in order to make Shakespeare commercially profitable you must have a sufficiently strong interest in him. In our country religion is still more commercialized but religion is there.'

That, as I see it, is the kernel of the matter. If people and towns flourish on religion in India it is because religion is a living thing in the country. Nobody flourishes on Kalidasa, however heavy he might be as a brick to throw at Englishmen when they talk about Shakespeare.

What surprised and at the same time delighted me still more was his vogue on the stage. The world's greatest writers can be the world's greatest bores. It is only when a man tries to read Shakespeare as he reads a modern novel that he feels how strangely distant and even absurd Shakespeare can be. But in contemporary England he seems to have become popular entertainment. Englishmen had not degraded the old play-wright, actor, and stage manager into a mere author.

I went to see *As You Like It* at the Old Vic on the day following that of my arrival, and when I took my seat the auditorium was already full. It was the seventeenth performance of the play in less than a month. It will be pointed out that the Old Vic is a repertory theatre whose business is to produce the classics. But men are more obstinate than horses, they cannot be even taken to the water, far less made to drink. A subsidized national theatre can give performances of the classics, but neither it nor anybody else can make people buy tickets unless they want to. Yet they *were* buying tickets.

I saw it being done in a very impressive manner at Stratford. I had gone out for my walk before six in the morning, and when returning I was astonished to see a large crowd before the Memorial Theatre. What were they doing there? When I came nearer I was even more astonished to find that men and women were sleeping on the ground under blankets with rucksacks as pillows. They had spent the night there in the open and in the cold in order to queue up for tickets, in fact they were sleeping in a queue. People do such a thing only when they get their money's or trouble's worth of enjoyment, they do not do it out of a sense of duty to culture.

What struck me even more powerfully was the behaviour of the audience during the performances. Here was a set of playgoers who need not have been playgoers at all but only film-viewers, but who were not only at a Shakespeare play but taking him in directly and naturally. I kept my eyes and ears partly open for the audience. It seemed to be composed of ordinary middle-class people, who in no way answered my preconceived notion of what a Shakespeare scholar or enthusiast should look like.

Nevertheless they were unmistakably showing their appreciation of the play, of the gorgeous Elizabethan rhetoric by close attention though they did not carry tablets, and of the vivacious Elizabethan jokes, some of them decidedly bawdy, by loud laughter. Critics have always been somewhat embarrassed by these jokes, and they have tried to explain them away by saying that Shakespeare was compelled to put them in to please his boisterous and coarse clientele. Even the robust Dr Johnson said that 'Shakespeare sacrifices virtue to convenience, and is so much more careful to please than to instruct, that he seems to write without any moral purpose'. Yet a modern audience, which could be expected to be squeamish by Elizabethan or even eighteenth-century standards, was finding the jokes quite acceptable. There was, however, to be another surprise. At the end of the play Rosalind came forward and spoke the epilogue:

> 'I am not furnished like a beggar,' [she said, pointing to her beautiful robes], 'therefore to beg will not become me: my way is to conjure you; and I'll begin with the women. I charge you, O women, for the love you bear to men, to like as much of this play as please you: and I charge you, O men, for the love you bear to women—as I perceive by your simpering, none of you hates them—that between you and the women the play may please. If I were a woman I would kiss as many of you as had beards that pleased me, complexions that liked me and breaths that I defied not: and I am sure, as many as have good beards or good faces or sweet breaths, will, for my kind offer, when I make curtsy, bid me farewell.'

The question arose in my mind—what had made a contemporary producer kept that bit of typical stage trick of the Elizabethan age? Rosalind was now a woman, and no longer a boy. But there was applause, and I heard some simpering myself. So the question was quickly disposed of. The same thing happened at Stratford. At the end of the performance of *Twelfth Night* the clown, Feste, sang the epilogue:

> *When that I was and a little tiny boy,*
> *With hey, ho, the wind and the rain,*
> *A foolish thing was but a toy,*
> *For the rain it raineth every day.*

Again the audience applauded. This performance was not received very enthusiastically by the dramatic critics, although John Gielgud was the producer and Laurence Olivier and Vivien Leigh were in the cast. Some of them found fault with the interpretation, and one critic said that the very beauty of the décor had distracted attention from the psychological situations. I had not seen any performance on a public stage before going to England, and I was enchanted not only with *Twelfth Night*, but with every play I saw. It was a delight to feast one's eyes on the lovely spectacles, and to hear English spoken. I had no idea that the language sounded so beautiful. I can still hear Rosalind saying, 'And I for no woman'. That scene was done like a vocal quartet in an opera.

So, when some days later I had a talk with a very cultured Frenchman in London about this performance, I mentioned the criticism to him. He promptly replied, 'What could it be besides a spectacle? The book was so fantastic or even absurd.' I was inclined to share this view. Whatever might be the stage history of the play and more especially of Malvolio's part, I did not think that there was much scope for psychological profundity in acting *Twelfth Night*. Even now I do not think that Shakespeare is profound in the modern sense of being accessible only with effort. He was perfectly intelligible to his contemporaries in the light of what they already had in their head and heart, as Aeschylus, Sophocles, and Euripides were to the Athenians. In any case, the producers and actors at Stratford had tried to please, and pleased the modern audience was.

Still, the main question remains unanswered. Why does Shakespeare appeal to a modern audience? No Englishman, and I have asked many, has been able to give me a satisfactory answer. Usually they say that at the Old Vic and at Stratford you have the best representation of Shakespeare by the best actors and producers. But that does not explain why the best producers and actors concern themselves with him. The immediate explanation I gave to myself was that the English people remain basically Elizabethan and have always been so. Afterwards I discovered that there is also something more in it.

The question raised by Shakespeare in England faced me in a much more extreme and intractable form in France. As I was walking along the Quai Malaquais, my eyes were suddenly arrested by a placard on a kiosk, which showed that Racine's *Athalie* was on at the Salle Richelieu of the Comédie-Francaise. I rushed back to the hotel and got a seat booked. When I entered the theatre in the evening I found the attendance to be even greater than at the Old Vic and the Memorial Theatre. Even Frenchmen were surprised when I told them about it. To non-French hearers *Athalie* sounds like continuous ranting, without any concession to love, humour, or any other human emotion. It remains throughout on the plane of Hebrew religious exultation, as embodied in classical French rhetoric.

The producer had made no secret of it. As I read in the programme notes: 'After reading the most dazzling psychological and philosophic acrobatics of the grammarians, polemicists, commentators, ecclesiastics, authors, and artists on the fabulous personages of this sumptuous epic, I have come back to the Bible and Racine. *Athalie* is one of the most beautiful paraphrases of the Old Testament. We are in a world in which man meets the Eternal. It is, to my thinking, a tragedy of the Hebrew character.'

All this and more from Mme Vera Korene, who produced the play and in addition acted the part of Athalie, which Sarah Bernhardt used to take, with the utmost distinction. For this play, obsolete by the standards of all Indian readers of Western literature, new stage sets and costumes had ben designed and made at enormous expense, and new music written. It was the 530th performance of the play at the Comédie-Francaise.

It was beautifully presented. I had seen some very fine décor and costumes in England and elsewhere in France, but for beauty and nobility combined this Racine play surpassed all the rest. For the sake of the spectacle in red and gold, white and gold, blue and gold, and in the case of one character in green, I would have gladly missed rows and rows of legs in any ballet. And of course, the acting and elocution were superb. The whole play remains before my mind's eye, but one scene comes back most readily. It is the scene in which the chorus sings:

> *O promesse! ô menace! ô ténébreux mystére!*
> *Que de maux, que de biens sont prédits tour à tour!*
> *Comment peut-on avec tant de colère*
> *Accorder tant d' amour?*

'What was the relation between a modern civilized people and their classics?' I asked myself. Frenchmen could not answer the question any more to my satisfaction than Englishmen. But as in the one case, so in the other, I succeeded in finding the answer by myself.

II

CULTURE BEGINS AT HOME

ANOTHER AMUSEMENT OF THE English people which must be given its place in their contemporary cultural life is the growing habit of visiting the country houses. Ever greater numbers of them are showing this new interest, though it is not always easy to satisfy it. There is a fairly high admission fee, 2s.6d., with another shilling for the garden in some cases, to which has to be added the cost of transport, meals, guidebooks, and souvenirs. As the English friend who took me to Albury Park said, 'Mr Chaudhuri, we cannot see these places as often as we wish to, because for a man with a family one visit means the greater part of a pound.' Nevertheless, in actual fact, immense numbers do visit them. When seeing Knole I was told that on Easter Monday more than a thousand people had come, and the guides were quite exhausted taking them round.

Here, too, I will not condemn the commercialization. Perhaps a few owners, or at all events their agents, practise the art of advertisement to a point which is perilously near angling. But so far as I could see none of the places were spoilt by being thrown open to visitors, and those which were in the hands of the National Trust were being protected from museumization. As for the owners they too had not come to any harm, and if some of them just disclosed a streak of simony, they could put forward a strong plea. When those who have not got such houses impoverish those who have, play up class prejudice from below, try to disassociate the Throne from them, gloat over their downfall, and at the same time rush to their houses to gape at their possessions and way of living, the owners are bound to exact their toll. But it is not really necessary to be so cynical about either of the parties. People went to see the country houses before the custom of charging a fee was introduced, and the new practice has not made much difference to the spirit of showing or seeing.

But why do people come to see them? Even though not as remote from contemporary interests as Shakespeare is, they are still things apart. One motivation of a practical order must be ruled out altogether, and that is the wish to get ideas about building, furnishing, and living in such places. Even historical interest in them or the families did not seem to be very strong, because many of the visitors had to be supplied with such information. Those who went to see them appeared to derive some immediate and direct satisfaction from the mere sight of the houses and their contents. I could plainly see that they were interested in the house as a building, in the park and the gardens, in the collection of furniture, pictures, and *objets d'art*. Among all this it was possible to make many interesting discoveries. I made a very unexpected one and wrote the following letter about it to the Editor of *The Times*, who printed it in his issue of 10 May 1955:

DIWAN-I-AM PANELS

Sir, I am sure a link that I observed between the Diwan-i-Am in Delhi and Penshurst Place will interest your readers. Every visitor to the Red Fort in Delhi must have noticed the *pietra dura* panels behind the throne platform in the Diwan-i-Am, among which there is one representing Orpheus with the beasts. It has been generally believed that these are of Italian and probably Florentine origin, though some have regarded them as Indian for no apparent reason.

While visiting Penshurst Place, in the Tapestry Room, I saw a cabinet with seventeen *pietra dura* panels of exactly the same design and in the same materials, namely, black marble and coloured stone, depicting as in Delhi, birds and flowers. I also saw in Warwick Castle a box with four such panels. I was told that the Penshurst Place cabinet is of Florentine origin and workmanship dating around 1640. I think that settles the question of the provenance of the Diwan-i-Am panels once and for all. Yours etc.

I was so excited when I saw them that I cried out, 'Why, we have exactly the same sort of panels in the Diwan-i-Am of Delhi!' It was probably the first time that so un-English a word had been uttered in the home of the Sidneys. So an English lady, who was among the visitors, came up to me and observed, 'You bring the breath of the wide world into this place!' I immediately wrote to my son to send me the colour transparencies of the Delhi panels and when I got them, sent one to Penshurst Place for comparison. My letter was not published until I had left London for Paris, and a most interesting letter from a lady in London was forwarded to me there, in which she informed me that her family too possessed a similar cabinet. I am sorry to say that I did not reply to her even after returning to India. East of Suez we disregard the commandment about replying to letters, but I hope that if the lady who wrote the letter sees these lines she will accept my apologies.

But however interesting such minor discoveries may be, the houses do not survive to provide these alone. I made a much more important one connected with English politics. I had always wondered how and from where Burke had got the idea for the famous passage: 'We have given to our frame of polity the image of a relation in blood; binding up the constitution of our country with our dearest domestic ties; adopting our fundamental laws into the bosom of our family affections; keeping inseparable, and cherishing with the warmth of all their combined and mutually reflected charities, our state, our hearths, our sepulchres, and our altars.' I found the answer in the country houses. I am not surprised either that Burke, dogged by poverty, debts, and anxieties all through life, built a country house for himself. Here is a picture of the making of politics in a country house at the end of the last century:

'After dinner we went into what I do think was the most fascinating room I ever saw in a house—great or small—one of the libraries, lined with well-bound books on white enamelled shelves, with a few, but not too many knick-knacks lying about, and all illuminated with the soft radiance of many clusters of wax candles. A picture to remember: Spencer with his noble carriage and fine red beard; Mr G. seated on a low stool, discoursing as usual, playful, keen, versatile; Rosebery saying little, but now and then launching a pleasant *mot*; Harcourt cheery, expansive, witty.'

And again on the next day:

'We met in the famous room where all the sovereign treasures of the bibliomaniacs are—the Caxtons, the Mazarin Bible, the Mainz Psalter; prizes acquired by an ancestor from funds procured by sale of land from Wimbledon to Hyde Park Corner. . . . Rosebery took up a book and turned it sedulously over, only interjecting a dry word now and then. Harcourt not diffuse.' Politics against the background of incunabula, to be followed the next morning by politics against the Pink: 'Spencer came into my room betimes in his pink, to return letters and say good-bye. He was off for a fourteen-mile drive to the meet, and the rain pouring.'

That explains to me why Ramsay MacDonald, even after country-house politics was wholly dead, pursued its glamour in a nationalized country house. Since English politics ceased to be made in the country houses it has wholly changed its character, for in politics the successor to the aristocrat is not the so-called common man of democracy, but the bureaucrat.

For those who have a feeling for history these houses are what haunted houses are for those who love ghosts. The friend who took me to Knole and Penshurst Place wrote the following letter to me after a visit to Kenwood House a year later:

'I had been thinking of you a day or two earlier when I happened to visit Kenwood House in brilliant sunshine after a light fall of snow, when it stood out in the distance looking like the last eighteenth-century villa on the face of the moon. I wish I could show it to you in that peculiar super-charged daylight.

'As it happened, I had just been reading the new edition of Margaret Jourdain's and her friend's account of their vision seen in Paris in the early 1900's, when these two serious Oxford ladies accidentally walked into the wrong dimension, and in broad daylight but uncanny silence saw a number of people, buildings, rocks, and trees, which hadn't actually been visible there for more than a century.

'Thinking of this I was wondering whether Kenwood doesn't in fact have all the original people and surroundings visible, perhaps on a certain day in every year or century, if only one knows how to get into the right frame of mind.

'Just then a hansom cab passed slowly across the facade, from one end of the terrace to the other. At that distance it was just distinguishable. Moving gently forward, so as not to break the spell, and keeping my eyes on the terrace (which looked dead and deserted instead of being crowded with people as it usually is on a fine Saturday morning), I saw two stout white horses come padding along, in the wake of the hansom, drawing a little vehicle of a kind I had only seen in old engravings: two seats facing forward, completely boxed in with glass windows, old cabbage-faced coachman in front, and inside a *figure*, a *personage*, someone of the calibre of Palmerston or the Duke of Wellington, sitting bolt upright in a heavy travelling coat—a Prime Minister profile with a great, heavy, nineteenth-century nose—and on the back of the chariot, phaeton, curricle (what was its name?), stains where the rain had melted a thick coating of dust and caused it to run down and then dry up again in the snowy sunlight. This suggested a journey about long enough to have lasted from Whitehall to Kenwood.

'Drawing nearer and looking around I saw that there were people about—certainly twenty couples in the lawn-like field running down to the lake. All the men were in top hats with heavy overcoats; the ladies were elderly, with travelling bonnets and cloaks like the pictures of Mrs Gladstone or earlier still. Behind the trees two heavy top-hatted figures with immense breadth of shoulders and military cloaks stamped up and down as if waiting for the protagonists in a duel, while a lady in a long close-fitting dress down to the ground clasped and unclasped her hands as if waiting too, with a more poignant interest than either of the men.

'A voice loud and clear as that of the Archangel Gabriel said, "We are going to shoot, so would that gentleman please stand back, right back?" But nobody fired a shot. Instead, yet another strange vehicle appeared—a Rolls car with a film camera fixed on with steel scaffolding, and five 1956 faces looking out of the top.'

Yet the romance of history is only an incidental interest in the country houses. My friend, whose letter I have quoted, used to have his falling asleep delayed in childhood by the discussion of food and wine between his father and George Saintsbury, which came wafting in from the dining-room. He remains capable of hallucinations which do not visit the general run of Englishmen. For them, I think, the houses suggest moods which belong to our times, however long they might have been brooded on in the past, moods which are incredibly homely and yet infinitely gracious. If an Englishman or Englishwoman wants today to be lifted out of the ordinariness of his or her daily life, and to carry back to it some *douceur de vivre* captured in the spirit, they can do no better than see these houses. After I had felt this myself I came upon a passage in John Stuart Mill's *Autobiography* which said exactly the same thing. Here it is:

'From 1814 to 1817 Mr Bentham lived during half of each year at Ford Abbey, in Somersetshire (or rather in a part of Devonshire surrounded by Somersetshire), which intervals I had the advantage of passing at that place. This sojourn was, I think, an important circumstance in my education. Nothing contributes more to nourish elevation of sentiments in a people, than the large and free character of their habitations. The middle-age architecture, the baronial hall, and the spacious and lofty rooms, of this fine old place, so unlike the mean and cramped externals of English middle-class life, gave the sentiment of a larger and freer existence, and were to me a sort of poetic cultivation....'

I would only add:

> *If this belief from heaven be sent,*
> *If such be Builder's holy plan,*
> *Have I not reason to lament*
> *What* flats *have made of Man?*

But in any case the English people are trying to bring into their flats sensations of more spacious habitations.

The passage from Mill shows that by the beginning of the nineteenth century, and perhaps much earlier than that, the country houses as a class had already come to stand for a definite quality in living. But there also seems to have been an earlier age of quarrels and rivalries among them, when the *palazzo* was being imported into the English countryside. The opening lines of Ben Jonson's poem on Penshurst Place illustrate this very clearly:

> *Thou art not*, PENSHURST, *built to envious show,*
> *Of touch, or marble; nor canst boast a row*
> *Of polish'd pillars, or a roofe of gold:*
> *Thou hast no lantherne, whereof tales are told;*
> *Or stayre, or courts; but stand'st an ancient pile,*
> *And these grudg'd at, art reverenc'd the while.*

The dig seems to be at Hatfield House. The date of the poem agrees with the date of the completion of that house. 'Touch or marble' appears to refer to the black and white marble of the Marble Hall; the pillars may be the pilasters on the sides of the arches of the Armoury, which once were open, or they may be the six columns of the central section of the south front illustrating the Orders; the staircase and the lantern are, of course, both famous and obvious; but the other details are something of a problem. In any case, it seems probable that not much love was lost between the Sidneys and the Cecils, and a protégé of the former would represent the new family as upstarts.

Ben Jonson makes two other points about the superior claims of Penshurst Place. First, he says that though built of the stone of the country its walls 'are reared with no man's ruin, no man's grone'. Then comes a really striking tribute:

> *These*, PENSHURST, *are thy praise, and yet not all.*
> *Thy lady's noble, fruitfull, chaste withall.*
> *His children thy great lord may call his owne:*
> *A fortune, in this age, but rarely knowne.*

When I saw the charming picture of Lady Sidney with her

six children in the Solar and stood before it full of admiration, I had not read the poem, and therefore I did not know what, in the estimation of the poet, was the special distinction of Barbara, née Gamage, and the lovely cherubs. Even the copious references to horns in Elizabethan literature had not led me to think that the joke was as well-founded in fact as Ben Jonson gravely suggests.

But these quarrels have now passed into history, and all the country houses stand today for about the same expression of the art of living. That is to say, Ben Jonson's final tribute to Penshurst is now applicable to all:

> Those proud, ambitious heaps, and nothing else,
> May say, their lords have built, but thy lord dwells

The antithesis is no longer valid, because in all of them their lords *dwell.*

I cannot understand why Sarah Higgins, the country girl whom the Earl of Exeter married and brought to Burghley House near Stamford in Lincolnshire, died of the magnificence of her new home. Even I, a Hindu who had lived all his life in the most primitive of surroundings, felt that I should be perfectly at home if I had to live even in the most grandiose of them, because they have acquired on the one hand an ineffable simplicity, and on the other a curious power to raise everyone who comes to them to their own level without effort and without self-consciousness. They still remain grand, but they are also humble. To me it seemed that in them the distinction between Paolo Veronese and Carlo Crivelli had been obliterated.

I felt this most strongly in the dining-rooms, of which I saw a few very well-laid ones. I thought that in such rooms it would be an intrusion even to be a gourmet. After dining on the most recherché menus and drinking the choicest vintages at these tables one could rise from them only in forgetfulness of all that had preceded and say with a glad and grateful heart: The Lord be thanked for having given us this day our daily bread.

I would say that the large numbers of English people whom I saw in these houses felt in the same way, though perhaps they did not bring to bear on their experience the detached analysis which was natural in me because I had been brought up in the traditions of a wholly different civilization.

III

ADVENTURES OF A BROWN MAN IN SEARCH OF CIVILIZATION

DURING MY STAY IN the West, short as it was, I met a situation that very much surprised me, for what I could not see there was today's Europe of our conception. It is the Europe on which the Public Service Commission in India sets the stiffest imaginable questions and to which, therefore, before the examination or interview, some of our acutest young brains devote some weeks of hectic cramming. This is also the Europe in which our intellectuals are interested to the exclusion of everything else. Without putting too fine a point on it, this Europe may be defined as the Europe of politico-economic tripe. The West, which has given us both politics and economics, can now have the satisfaction of seeing these ugly little cuckoo-twins throwing out the young of one of the wisest old birds in creation and usurping their nest. Englishmen will be amused, perhaps a little put out of countenance also, to learn that the Mother Church of these fanatical converts is the London School of Economics. Hinduism will one day have to settle its scores with this institution.

Unfortunately, I cannot say that this Europe of current politics and economics does not exist. But at all events it does so in a dimension of reality which is not perceptible through the senses. One has to make a special effort to discover it, whereas there is another Europe which is tangible everywhere. It is not simply that you can see this other Europe if you want to, you cannot escape it even if you do not. This is the Europe of European civilization, which is entwined with the contemporary existence of the European peoples, influencing and shaping it in every way, and being accepted as part and parcel of their ordinary life.

Whatever may happen in the future, European civilization remains as much of the present as of the past. In fact, it is so omnipresent that if I had to call anything today's Europe, I would rather attach this label to the Europe of culture than to that of politics and economics. In the West it seemed impossible to separate the life of the present from the historic past, or to overlook the basic elements of Western civilization in the preoccupation with passing matters.

All this will seem too obvious to need mention unless I explain the cultural situation to which I am accustomed in my country. India is a land of ancient and massive civilizations, but the universal recognition of this fact has enabled us to repudiate the contract with the past. As a Hindu and also as a student of history I have always wanted to meet the civilization of ancient India—to understand its nature and to feel it as a living reality. Considering how traditional we still remain, this should not have been difficult. Yet I can only read about it, or attempt to reconstruct it by a painful exercise of inference and imagination. I can never be sure that I have captured its spirit.

For the great majority of my countrymen their historic civilization is a culture in the anthropologist's sense of the word. It has been reduced to its simplest to become a more or less inert psychological environment, in which they live as fish do in water. As for those Indians who have imbibed the notion of civilization from their Western education, their ancient culture is a thing to throw at the heads of foreigners, never to be carried on their own shoulders, where it is felt as a burden. Our men of culture practise it in the abstract, as modernist painters practise abstract art. Their cultural consciousness is a part of their nationalism.

I hope it will now be seen why I make so much of the situation I found in the West. Let me, however, give some illustrations. When I was in Paris, I noticed every day a large crowd before the Orangerie. Sometimes the queue was several scores of people long, and it hardly seemed to shorten. These men and women were coming to see the exhibition of French paintings from David to Toulouse-Lautrec in the American collections, which were on loan and being shown under the slogan *Salut a la France*. The entrance fee was 200 francs, the catalogue cost 100 francs, and there were other incidental expenses. But these hardly seemed to have any effect on the attendance.

At the same time a political conference was being held a few hundred yards away, at the Quai d'Orsay. It came in the way of my seeing the Salle de l'Horloge, and therefore I had to take note of it—otherwise I should have ignored it. But I could not possibly have overlooked the exhibition. So I also said, '*Salut a la France*, for teaching her children to respect the distinction which exists between the things that are God's, and those that are Caesar's.' India without politics is a bare expanse of petty worldliness, Europe without politics is by far the most attractive part of Europe.

I found the same situation in England. If any nation of our times has the right to put forward the economic excuse for neglecting culture, it is the English people. The wealthiest country in the world has lost the greater part of its wealth; the richest families have become relatively poor; there is the crushing load of taxation without proportionate benefit for those who are bearing the greater share of its burden; last of all, nothing that they can do seems to promise an end to the economic torture. Reading about all this, I had expected that the economic situation would be endangering cultural life. I did not indeed think that the highest expressions of English civilization had become museum exhibits, but I did assume that they would be found to be surviving as more or less exclusive activities in more or less exclusive circles, in short, as the esoteric interests of a dwindling *élite*.

What I saw was, however, the opposite. I have already spoken about the popularity of two of the highest expressions of English civilization, Shakespeare and the country houses. I could easily give many other examples. On any day I could have my choice of any music that had made musical history, any ballet that had made history in choreography, any painting and sculpture famous in the history of art, or half a dozen buildings that had their place in the history of architecture. On the third day after my arrival in England I walked into the National Gallery all by myself. As I passed through the aisle formed by the Italian Primitives I was dazzled by their splendour. I had a notion that I knew something about European painting. I found out how mistaken I was. What I knew was not a shadow of the reality.

It is only those who do not possess collections like the National, Tate, and Wallace who can realize that to have built them up is in itself an achievement in civilization. At Cambridge I felt very indignant that of the many acquaintances of mine who had been to the University, not one had told me about the Fitzwilliam Museum. This and the Ashmolean at Oxford are just as important as any college for a man who cares to lead a civilized life. These collections can indeed be overpowering and, as a French museologist has said, a cause of nervous strain to a cultivated tourist who is torn between his desire to look long enough at a particular work and his fear of missing some of the other masterpieces. But they were never meant to make a man cultured in the course of one visit, as I found a fair number of people trying to be in the biggest ones, especially the Louvre and the Vatican. Some of the visitors were hardly looking, but scribbling frantically all the time.

I adopted the easiest and pleasantest way of seeing the galleries and museums. 'No obligation to see anything at all,' I said to myself to give my senses confidence; after that I made a rapid general survey, and last of all looked as long as I wished at a small number of things I wanted specially to see. To give one or two examples, upon my first visit to the British Museum, which can be an anaesthetic if seen in the wrong way, I selected the Elgin Marbles, Assyrian sculptures, and because I was interested in the early history of the Bible and its manuscripts, also the Codex Sinaiticus, Codex Alexandrinus, and the Lindisfarne Gospels. What pleased me most was that without looking for it I came upon the statue of Demeter, which I had been wanting to see since I was a schoolboy. As I wrote within an hour to my family: 'It was a happy omen that the first things I saw were a statue of Marcus Aurelius and of Demeter, the famous B.M. Demeter. She is divine. Then I went through all the sculpture galleries, seeing the Elgin Marbles....All of it is on a stupendous scale. The metopes from the Parthenon are much bigger than I thought they would be.' I saw Magna Carta incidentally. Last of all, I went upstairs and sought out the Sutton Hoo treasures.

In the National Gallery, besides some dozen paintings I was specially interested in, I looked for *The Nativity* by Piero della Francesca in the room in which the cleaned paintings were hung I had always liked that picture in reproductions, and I was also curious about a recent controversy. I had been told in Delhi by a European friend of mine, who had seen the painting both before and after the cleaning, that it had been spoiled by the process. I could not, of course, form any opinion on the question at dispute, but I immensely liked the painting as it was.

I found a very attractive blue in it, which I had not seen in the reproductions. Afterwards in Delhi I met a distinguished art critic, who had once been in charge of the National Gallery, and I put the matter to him. He told me that most definitely it was not spoiled. There the question must rest, so far as I am concerned.

I must also refer to one result of my first visit to the National Gallery. It immediately confirmed my liking for Claude Lorrain, my dislike for Rubens—which became a grievance because for the first time I realized the greatness of his technical skill; it also provided a wholly unexpected discovery—Poussin. I had not been able to see much in this master before, but after seeing the originals I acquired a very great respect for him, which was deepened further in the Louvre. I thought he employed a very attractive red and blue.

But when I spoke about the ease with which things of cultural interest could be found in England, I was not thinking only of London. The provincial towns surprised me very much. Take Bristol, for example. I now know what Bristolians think of their city, but before I saw it and a little of the life it offered I thought of it only as a commercial city—and that too not in the sense in which Florence and Venice, Amsterdam and Antwerp, or the Hanseatic towns were commercial, but in that other sense in which, taking Napoleon's jibe too seriously, we thought of the English people as shopkeepers. To that Bristol's rejection of Burke as its member had added a political prejudice. So when I found that the British Council had put it in my programme as the first provincial city to be visited by me, I was somewhat perplexed.

However, a visit to the Georgian House in Great George Street revealed to me that even the shopkeeper had his standards. But still I found it difficult to understand why, by any standards not its own, Bristol should have one of the finest theatres in England, and why when I was there this theatre should have been giving performances of a French play, Jean Giraudoux's *Intermezzo*, the theme of which has been summarized by M. Jean-Louis Vaudoyer of the French Academy in these formidable words: 'La pièce est l'histoire d'une "amitié invisible", nouée entre une jeune fille que la vie n'a pas encore touchée et une ombre errante, rappelée des portes de la mort par la force et la foi de cette rêveuse éveillée. Mais les réalités de l'existence défendent à ce rêve de durer bien longtemps: le mort suscité par une "sorcellerie naturelle" disparaît lorsque le coeur de la jeune fille se laisse émouvoir par l'amour d'un mortel; le miracle n'est plus permis.'

I had not read this exegesis when I saw the play at Bristol. So, when the friend who had taken me to the play asked me what I thought of it, I replied, 'It seemed to be a close contest between death and French rhetoric.' But he murmured, 'That fellow, the ambivalent one...,' referring to The Droguiste, and stopped short without completing the sentence, which showed that he had felt what the piece was meant to convey—man's ambivalence between life and death.

By a most interesting coincidence I saw the same play in Paris, at one of the best theatres for contemporary plays, the Marigny, where it was staged by the well-known Compagnie Renaud-Barrault, with Simone Valere as Isabelle. I would not say that the production was on a lower level at Bristol, though certainly in French the play had a different flavour.

At Oxford, too, I saw a modern French play, and that was Jean Anouilh's *Bal des Voleurs*. It began as such an extravagance that the head of an Oxford College whispered in my ears, 'Mr Chaudhuri, do not be put out if you are mystified by it. We are not understanding it either.' But from the second act onwards the story began to clear up, and the end quite justified the play's claim to be regarded as one of Anouilh's '*pieces roses*'.

I was invariably lucky in my quests. I had been wishing to hear the Second Symphony of Beethoven for years, and it was in the programme when I went to a concert at the Festival Hall. The very evening I arrived at Cambridge I was taken to hear Handel's *Messiah*, sung by the Cambridge Philharmonic Society. It was very beautifully done. People say that the *Messiah* is a favourite in England. This again goes no further than saying that Shakespeare attracts Englishmen. It does not explain why Handel appeals in these days as only film music or jazz is supposed to.

But my real surprise, one which delighted me most, was over the discovery that I could satisfy some of my out-of-the-way interests with the greatest ease. Of these, I shall mention only one or two. In 1923 or 1924 Elkin Mathews and Marrot had published a sumptuous folio edition of *Jane Eyre*, with lithographs by a French artist. I formed an intense longing to buy it when I read the review, but I could not then afford the five guineas at which it was priced, and I never heard about it afterwards. However, when I walked into the Charlotte Bronte exhibition in the British Museum, which was being held to celebrate the hundredth anniversary of her death, I came upon the selfsame folio, looking as beautiful as I had imagined it would.

I had also wanted to see some at least of the more famous incunabula, especially the Forty-two Line Bible and some of the Aldines. I did not expect that I should be able to do so without applying for special permission either to the British Museum or the Bodleian. But, as it happened, exhibitions of early printed books were being held at both libraries just at that time, and I was able to satisfy my curiosity.

One early Aldine I had been specially keen to see. It was the *Hypnerotomachia Poliphili*, published in 1499 and illustrated with beautiful wood engravings. I had come to know about it from Herbert Furst's book, *The Modern Woodcut*, published in 1924, in which one of its illustrations (about which I shall say something presently) was reproduced. When I saw the original I thought that it was the most beautifully printed and illustrated book I had ever seen.

This particular Aldine had an additional interest for me on account of the solution it offered in the illustration to which I have just referred, to a literary problem which has always been present in my mind. It is this: Does a literary man write only from direct experience of life, or does he see life through books and is inspired by books as well? Take, for instance, the stanza in Gray's *Elegy*:

> *There at the foot of yonder nodding beech*
> *That wreathes its old fantastic roots so high,*
> *His listless length at noontide would he stretch*
> *And pore upon the brook that babbles by.*

What was the source from which Gray got this image? He himself wrote to Horace Walpole that he sometimes lay under one of the Burnham beeches. But he was not the man to go by his personal experience alone, as Wordsworth with his original and individual approach to poetry always did. There must have been some literary model for Gray. The obvious one was the image of Jaques:

> *Today my lord of Amiens and myself*
> *Did steal behind him as he lay along*
> *Under an oak, whose antique root peeps out*
> *Upon the brook that brawls along this wood.*

But where did Shakespeare himself get it from? I discovered from the illustration in the *Hypnerotomachia* that the idea of the mooning scholar-poet had come out of the Renaissance. It showed a man in cap and gown lying at full length under a tree, intently gazing on something before him, and perhaps, like Jaques, 'moralizing the spectacle'. It is not improbable that besides being familiar with the idea, both Shakespeare and Gray had seen this particular illustration, if not in the Aldine itself, at all events in the French translation with the same type of illustrations, which was published in 1554.* This to my mind proved conclusively that, like painting, literature also observes a swinging rhythm between natural and man-made models.

The things I have been singling out for mention may be set down as very special interests. Some of them are, but that would not invalidate the point I am wishing to make about the general character of the cultural life of the English people. These things were not on view for me, *pour mes beaux yeux*, they were meant for the natives. If in Shakespeare and the country houses my interests coincided with theirs, in the case of these things their

---

* After writing the above I learnt that an English translation of the *Hypnerotomachia* was published in 1592, and so I wrote to my son to go to the British Museum and find out the particulars. I got the following reply from him: 'The English translation by R.D. (supposed to be Sir Robert Dallington), done for Sir Philip Sidney and addressed to Robert Devereux, Earl of Essex, was printed in London by Simon Waterson and sold at the East Gate of St Paul's. It has got rather debased copies of the original illustrations, not quite so many, but all the principal ones are reproduced. I also looked up another folio edition of the *Hypnerotomachia*, printed at Venice in MDXXXXV, autographed by Ben Jonson, and bought in 1642 by a student whose signature appears on the cover. It is very heavily annotated in the margins, almost every word being translated and marked. This edition has also got all the principal illustrations. I think it is particularly interesting, and as it is autographed by Ben Jonson, it is very probable that the book was known among Shakespeare's circle of dramatists.'

This seems to confirm my supposition that Shakespeare may have seen the illustration. In the case of Gray the probability is not less.—N.C.C.

interests must have coincided with mine. There must have been a few thousand men and women who were interested in them, perhaps many more than those who read the novels of Jane Austen when they were first published and established her position. Therefore these things are admissible as evidence to prove the English people's interest in civilization.

At this point someone might ask me, 'What is civilization?' Although *he* might not wait for an answer, *I* will give one. At the end of the nineteenth century when mankind had taken a new leap towards material progress, advanced thinkers identified civilization with soap, as the symbol of cleanliness. *Sanitas sanitatum, omnia sanitas*, they cried triumphantly. But the establishment of universal sanitation with universal suffrage has made the people of the West less confident. Finding that sanitation can co-exist with the most crushing forms of vulgarity or even rank barbarism of the mind, some of them are rushing to the extreme point of denying the idea of civilization altogether. I should like to reassure them by suggesting a new test for it, which I employed. It is the number and prosperity of the shops dealing in antiques, old books, and second-hand furniture. Judged by this test the people of England are very civilized, for I found these shops everywhere, stocking goods for all purses.

But for those who would not admit this as a criterion of civilization, I would set down another, which is more general. An Englishman as gardener is professing allegiance to his civilization in the same manner as he would have done if he were buying old prints, furniture, and books. The Chelsea Flower Show is as great an expression of English civilization in its way as is Shakespeare in his.

IV

KINDERGARTEN AND PEDAGOGY

It would seem that even if I have not actually fallen into it, I have slipped to the very brink of the pitfall against which I warned myself at the beginning, namely, taking too serious a view of the cultural life of the English people. But their attitude is somewhat of a puzzle to me. It cannot be said that they avoid solemnity at all costs and in everything. In fact, they can be almost priggishly solemn precisely in that thing over which other nations are playful, or at all events were, until the English example corrupted them. Of course, that is sport.

Young Englishmen who rebel against the tutor of the brain grovel abjectly at the feet of the tutor of the brawn. Here swotting is the thing. The whole nation has come to believe in the moral equivalents of play and sport, as a wholly non-functional, non-purposive, and specialized exercise of the muscles. They are under no biological compulsion to acquire the efficiency of a horse in the legs, of a hare in the wind, of a gibbon in the arm, or of a tiger in the paw, yet they have set their heart on attaining all these skills.

Thus, if anything can be called *la mystique anglaise*, it is sport. When the English people say, 'Play up! play up! and play the game!' I seem to see the gesture and hear the tones of the Frenchman who is reported to have cried out, 'La garde meurt, ne se rend pas!' They have even invented the absurd saying that the battle of Waterloo was won on the playing fields of Eton, totally forgetting the great contribution of their own thinkers to the science of logic, for they have failed to observe the true sequence of cause and effect—that winning at Waterloo was not the effect of playing at Eton, but both were effects in different directions of the same cause, which remains unobserved.

This illogicality did no harm so long as the English people were capable of trifling at Eton and fighting elsewhere. But now when the fight (in the political sense) seems to have gone out of the dogs it is making far too many people think that Wembley and Lord's are perfectly adequate substitutes for Blenheim and Waterloo. I do not like this seriousness, and I wish they could be as pleasant and relaxed in their sport as they are in their pursuit of culture.

Yet it is only common sense to recognize that such a highly civilized life as is theirs cannot be maintained without effort, thinking, method, and education, for old Caliban has become a greater seducer of mankind than even Satan himself. So there is plenty of all this in the behind-the-scenes of cultural life. The teachers in this sphere stand behind culture as chefs stand behind good living, and trainers and coaches behind sport. They have however, to perform their role very discreetly, because Englishmen tend to grow restive whenever they notice any deliberate instruction. That is why there are detractors of the Third Programme even among cultured Englishmen. As a result, the world of English culture has become divided between a kindergarten in the showrooms and a pedagogy in the backshops. I shall speak about the pedagogy first in order to earn the right to enjoy the kindergarten.

The first check on the quality of cultural life is exercised by the pupils themselves. Although the general run of Englishmen are always ready to applaud any performance, more especially a plucky failure, there also are a not negligible few who are never pleased with anything that has been achieved, however good it may be. They are able to find fault with every performance. The musical, dramatic, and art critics of the press are the shock troops of this Guards Division. Since my standards are somewhat lax and human I think that they have a weakness for carping, but I cannot blame them for this. I have seen how quickly standards begin to go down if even for once the rein is slackened and the whip thrown away. If I might paraphrase the cliché, eternal vigilance is the price a nation has to pay for keeping its civilization.

To come now to the men who are keeping cultural life going. These are easily divisible into three groups: the *entre-*

preneurs, the interpreters, and the popularizers whose real work is to proselytize, that is to say, bring into the fold of civilization those who are outside it. For each of these groups I have acquired real respect. Though feuds break out at times between the professional critics and the *entrepreneurs* of cultural activities, I would not say that the latter are in any way less exacting and painstaking, though they exercise their functions with sympathy. I shall set down for what it is worth the opinion of a layman that if technical excellence alone is to be considered, there never was a time when the level of execution in music, drama, painting, or any other field of culture stood higher. Some people even think that there is so much stress in these days on pure technique that insight and feeling are often lost in virtuosity. I could not form any opinion on that point, but even I could detect the amazing technical skill which lay behind every amusement.

I think I am also justified in thinking that the *haute vulgarisation* of the historic civilization of the English people is very competent. Its interpretation by university men and men of letters seems to be absolutely first-rate. The English Alexandrians are doing splendid service by making their civilization accessible to all. One day in the National Gallery I heard a lecturer explaining Constable's work. He was going into details of style and technique which formerly would have been addressed only to professionals.

Those who were devoting themselves to the work of conversion to civilization, the new missionaries of our times, were a very attractive set of men. I saw them at two adult education centres, one at Bristol and the other at Urchfont Manor, a pleasant Queen Anne house on the northern edge of Salisbury Plain. I shall quote what I wrote to my family after seeing the Bristol Centre: 'Then I went to see a young man who is in charge of an adult education centre here, and later I launched with him and his wife. There was a long-haired dachshund in the house, the first of this breed that I have seen in my life, called Monster, who as his master said had no colour prejudice, but kept a strict watch on me when I was left alone in the living room, which contained many sixteenth and seventeenth-century books, including a sixteenth-century French edition of Quintilian's *Orations.*' Originally an engineer, he was, as he told me, a product of the adult education movement himself. He was specializing on English literature of the seventeenth century. The Warden of Urchfont Manor was a university man who had turned to this kind of work.

I found the programmes of these two centres quite interesting. The course of lectures at Urchfont Manor included among many others the following subjects: Introduction to the opera; Myth, reason and reality; From author to public; A prospect of Germany; Painting in summer (practical); Archaeology, and so on and so forth. The Bristol centre had a number of long courses in twenty-four meetings, and among them were the following: Beethoven and the Viennese period; Modern English literature; The Mendips, a regional study based on a geographical survey of the area; Philosophy and religion; Life, work and ritual in antiquity.

If I considered all this very significant, I did not find the small practical aids given less striking. Upon my arrival in Bristol I was given two pamphlets, one entitled *What's on in Bristol* and the other *A Day in Bristol.* They gave pretty full information about what there was to see and hear in the town, ranging from art exhibitions to sporting events. Out of the list I could choose either a Bach recital or a wrestling match, and with the help of the little map printed in one of them I made my way early one morning from Clifton to St Mary Redcliffe without any guidance. For additional information I could go to the City Information and Advice Bureau. It is only those who have to wait for a cultural event over a period of months, who have to run from pillar to post to get news of it, and who have to be very rich or belong to privileged cliques to gain access to any, who can truly value this trouble-free cultural enjoyment.

But the immense effort that lay behind the organization of cultural life in England never obtruded itself in the actual presentation, where everything seemed to be natural and spontaneous. It was a great delight for me to see this, and an even greater pleasure to find that those who were seeking cultural enjoyment could bring an equally easy informality and even playfulness into it. It is to Bristol that I shall go again to illustrate this.

There I was introduced to the Dean of the Faculty of Arts of the University, a blind professor, whose vitality and courage amazed me. When he heard that I was in the town for a very short visit he invited me to come to the meeting of the Savage Club that evening. He thought it would interest me, and it did. As I reported to my people at home:

> 'Now, I am afraid I shall not be able to give you an adequate idea of the club meeting. The club is in an old sixteenth-century house, which is maintained as a period museum, and its own hall is a timbered barn type of room, with all sorts of weapons, heads of game, oil paintings, etc. The chairman sits at his table with a huge silver skull in front of him, and everybody calls fellow-members "Brother Savages!"
>
> 'There was no suggestion of spreeing anywhere, for all the Savages were well over forty, and many over sixty. But there was exuberance and jollity, and they sang, recited poetry, and made speeches. An exercise is always set in painting, and the subject is given exactly one and a half hours before the meeting, and those who want to compete have to finish a painting in oils, watercolour, *gouache*, or pastels within that period. About twenty-four pictures were submitted yesterday, and some received special mention.
>
> 'The visitors were formally introduced, and little speeches were made about them. At the end of the introductions they all shout the word "welcome" in a Red Indian language, for the club is regarded as a wigwam. I think I may have been the first Indian to be there. My professor friend said that he was very glad that I was in Bristol on a Wednesday, and another friend said that I had got a better idea of English life there in two hours than I could have elsewhere in two months.'

When a member asked me whether I would not like to see the pictures I went up and looked at them. If any of my many professional painter friends in India had done things like these I should have thought them very good indeed.

There is the same unpretentiousness in intellectual life, so far as it forms part of general culture. I could not see the more serious aspect of it, because that can be observed only by fellow-workers. But from what I saw of it in social intercourse I found that the English intellectual in company is different from the French *savant* in the salons. In France, however easy and sparkling the intellectual discussion may be, the style of social intercourse has to tune itself to what I would call the *diapason cérébral*, while in England the discussion has to lower itself to the lunch or dinner pitch. That came out in what my blind professor friend wrote to me after reading my autobiography: 'Time after time I wanted to rush off to you and say, "I thoroughly agree with you," or "I don't believe that." Indeed, at one time, I thought of making notes in order that in writing to you I could mention all the points that occurred to me, but the only way is really more discussion, preferably at the Savile Club, over a bottle of the best.'

This reminds me that at the Savile, while dining with him, I drank a very fine port of the 1927 vintage. Hearing of my interest in wines he presented me with a fine bottle of Pomerol. Sea voyages are unkind to good red wine, and I thought since I was travelling by air I should at last have a chance of drinking something exceptional, and I also promised my friend that I would carry back the bottle with me like a baby in its cradle. But after I had brought it safely across six customs benches, my youngest son dropped it from his hands in my bedroom and I had to see it smashed before my eyes.

I only wish I could match the informality. But that was not easy for me. After getting familiar with the notion of culture from the West we Hindus have developed an over-consciousness of culture. Besides, my own early initiation into culture was historical, and that too mostly from the French and German historians of civilization. When I was young, Indian students who cared about such things used to read about English literature in Taine, about civilization in Guizot, and about the Renaissance in Burckhardt. Though I also read some Buckle, that did not improve matters, for Buckle is the most un-English of English historians. It is significant that he knew eighteen languages and was one of the best chess-players of his time. In after life, however, I became interested in the art of living and approached cultural history and activities from a more human angle. Even so I do not think I have been wholly successful in shedding my early seriousness about cultural matters.

So all that I could do was to show an intensely sensuous absorption in cultural displays, without ever discussing them intellectually. I would only see and hear, and never talk. This may have redeemed my conduct. One friend who took me to see a very popular play, *Sailor, Beware!* at the Strand, must have observed this, for after I came back to India he wrote to me:

'A friend told me of a man who took a large sad-looking St Bernard dog into a cinema, and settled down with it beside him in a front seat to look at the film. At first the dog seemed bored, but after a time it brightened up, seeming to follow the story with intelligence, wagging its tail, uttering eloquent growls, etc. At the end the man sitting next to them said, "That is a remarkable dog. He really seemed to like the film." "Oh yes, he did," said the owner, "and the queer thing is that he hated the book!"'

My friend would feel outraged if I said that he wrote that with me in his mind. But I do hope that in the subconscious Freudian depths of his mind the dog and I merged in each other.

V

CHRISTIAN CIVILIZATION

THERE IS, HOWEVER, ONE region of the cultural life of the English people in which there is no question of anything but seriousness. It is occupied by religion. It must be widely known that the author of one of the supreme achievements of English culture, *Alice's Adventures in Wonderland*, was not only devoted to indices and surds, but also to religion. He was deeply distressed by the conduct of a friend who at a dinner in his rooms had repeated some remarks made by children about very sacred subjects on the assumption that since they were innocent when made by children who were unconscious of any irreverence they were also innocent when repeated by a grown-up person. 'The hearing of that anecdote', he wrote, 'gave me so much pain, and spoiled so much of the pleasure of my tiny dinner party, that I feel sure you will kindly spare me such in future.' Some Englishmen of today, who do not consider the humour of *Alice* to be Victorian, set down this seriousness to Victorianism. This discriminatory appraisement will simply not hold water. It has to be admitted that if the nonsense of *Alice* is national the religious susceptibility of Lewis Carroll is also national. Without it the book would have been a different kind of classic, something like *Candide* or *Gargantua and Pantagruel.*

I hope, however, that I am not giving offence to Englishmen by including religion in culture. There is no reason why I should. I wish very much indeed that I could also say something about the place of religion in the personal life of the English people, but I really had no opportunities for learning anything about that. Therefore I am compelled to restrict myself to what I saw. But that too was one of the major aspects of their religious life. Everybody recognizes that Christianity has been a great force behind the rise of Western civilization, and one of its earliest manifestations, the Anglo-Saxon, was intensely Christian. A very vivid way of realizing the difference which the new religion made to the life of these strong and young people is to think of Penda the Mercian and then of Alfred. Religion and culture have always intermingled in Europe, more so in England than anywhere else. This is in every elementary textbook, so if I also became conscious of it, there was no originality in my perception. Its only point of interest lies in the fact that it was suggested by a direct personal contact with contemporary affairs, and was not due to what I had read, all of which fortunately had gone out of my mind when I was there.

My introduction to the religious life of the English people began at Canterbury. There could be no fitter place for it. In the Cathedral a very learned canon explained to me what it stood for and symbolized. He considered the spirit which had created it, first, historically and then *sub specie aeternitatis*. He did not, however, say anything about the passing fragment of time in which we were living. The significance of the Cathedral for the present age, I could only feel from the atmosphere, and I felt it unprompted. Canterbury was not a tourists' town, and I think it was a mistake to call the bombings of 1942 'Baedeker raids'. The bombs did not burst merely on a four-star show-place, however ancient. They hit sensibilities which were very much deeper, and certainly went to convince the English people finally that there could be no compromise between Nazism and their way of life.

But I did not attend any religious service at Canterbury. The first one I attended was at Cambridge over Easter. I was fortunate in respect of the place of worship, for it was King's College Chapel. I went to see it one morning with a large number of visitors who had come to spend their holiday in the old university town, instead of going to a gay seaside resort. We were stopped at the entrance of the choir because a rehearsal was going to be held. I looked at the magnificent vault and the glowing stained glass, and suddenly heard a lovely voice singing a melody which rose to the lofty roof like a coil of incense smoke. I was told that it was the voice of a boy chorister. Its quality was different from that of any voice I had heard before, and only the previous night I had been listening to the whole of Handel's *Messiah*.

In the afternoon I came again, this time to evensong. My English friend, who had not intended to remain through the service but had come only to put me in my seat, stayed on, saying that it was a very moving experience. He was a literary critic by vocation. I had read so much about the decline of religious belief, falling church attendance, and ignorance of the Bible that I was surprised by the number of people I saw and no less by the absence of any mood which could be called non-devotional. So the old question which had arisen in my mind about Shakespeare posed itself again in a more insistent manner. What was it that had brought so many men and women to a church service?

Though the choir of the Chapel was famous, that could not have been the main inducement. In any case, nobody was treating the service as a song recital, nor was there any concession to that character in the singing itself, from which all traces of virtuosity had been taken away. I noticed the expression on the faces as people left the Chapel. There was no sudden break in the silence, either through resumption of conversation or footfalls. They went out with a grave and abstracted expression as if what they had gone through was still holding them in its grip. Nobody even cast a last look at the noble interior.

The next day was Easter Sunday, and I again went to the Chapel. This time the attendance was even greater than on the previous afternoon. Once again I felt the power of the service, and though I could not define in what it lay, I said to myself that if anywhere I, a Hindu, could think of becoming a Christian it was in such a place.

I attended other services at Stratford and Winchester which gave me the same impression. But I did not see any services outside the Anglican Church, and therefore I cannot say what effect they would have produced. I suppose Englishmen would have found a difference, but to me that would certainly not have been material. All Christian worship in England would have had the same appearance to me. Their spirit would have been common.

But what was that spirit? I never got any insight into it, and I never asked any Englishman what he was seeking in his religious observances or what he was getting out of them. I could only apply Hindu analogies, with which I was familiar, and they failed to enlighten me. For instance, I wondered if they went to a church as we went to a temple. We go to temples to look on the image of a divine potentate and to watch the ceremonials of his daily life, which are modelled on those of a king. We do indeed prostrate ourselves in awe before him, but that used to be done by the ancient Egyptians before the Pharaoh and by the Japanese before their Emperor. Modern Indians did that before Mahatma Gandhi, and do it now before Jawaharlal Nehru. Between these secular prostrations and the prostrations before the gods there is only a difference of degree and not of kind, because in India the most powerful political leadership is itself quasi-religious. But certainly the English people did not go to their churches to look on a Divine Ruler and his daily life.

However, temple cults, popular as they are, are no part of true Hinduism. None of our scriptures refers to them or lays on a Hindu the duty of going to a temple or worshipping an image. These cults were borrowed by the ancient Hindus from western Asia, and even after their adoption in India they and their gods, together with the habitations of these gods, retained the features they had in their homeland. The gods remained the same divine lords of cities as they were in western Asia: all the greater reason why there could be no resemblance between our temple worship and Christian worship, for Christianity had fought and triumphed over those very cults.

I then tried more specifically Hindu or Brahmanic forms of religious experience. True Hinduism in its most universally understood and practised aspect makes us accept the universe and requires us to make such a welfare universe of it with the help of the gods that any man-made welfare state can only be a pinchbeck imitation of it. Some of the welfare is thought of in purely worldly terms. In olden days kings turned to religion for the sake of conquest, for the preservation of their kingdom, and for the recovery of lost thrones; the merchant for wealth; the peasant for crops; and all for children, health, and prosperity. We do so still. This is the prayer to our Mother Goddess: 'Give me longevity, fame, good fortune, O Goddess, give me sons, wealth, and all things desirable.'

But a Hindu's pursuit of welfare in the world is not wholly materialistic, although materialism is an essential part of the Hindu religious outlook. Hinduism has kept the old economic gods in the pantheon so that economics might not drive religion out of the life of mankind altogether, as it is doing in the West. It is certainly less foolish, if not more sensible, to keep the two together than to set them at loggerheads. In Hinduism this has served to infuse a glow of spirituality into worldly prosperity and happiness, which are most desirable and at their best in a semi-sanctified state as the necessary preliminary to the triumph of Dharma, which in its turn is the realized and unrealized righteousness that keeps the world going. This is the typical Hindu concept which stands beyond the purely material aspect of the Hindu welfare universe. But all these basic aspirations of Hinduism were absent from the collective worship of the English people, which seemed to be inspired by a movement of the spirit leading away from the world.

Nor was there any trace in it of the third feature of our collective worship: namely, propitiation and coercion of the gods through offerings, sacrifices, and incantations, which create a gamut of moods from a propitious silence and super-magical tenseness to Dionysiac frenzy. In Hinduism it is not the dread Kali alone who exacts a bloody sacrifice from her worshippers, the benign Mother Goddess Durga requires this equally. But a Hindu has not to be a mere suppliant at the feet of his gods and goddesses. He can also assert the claims of mankind on the deities by scrupulously performing the duties which are in his part of the covenant. In the Hindu religion, somehow, status has been replaced by contract in the relationship between gods and men. Nowhere is this stated more clearly than in the Gita, which is almost a revealed scripture of Hinduism, though strictly speaking it is not one. About rituals it says:

With this prosper ye the gods
And let the gods prosper you;
Prospering one the other
Ye shall attain the highest welfare.
Gita, III-11 *(Tr. by* Edgerton)

There are, of course, many other facets of Hinduism, but those do not form part of collective worship and so do not come into comparison with what I saw of Christian worship in England, and even where the two did so, it will already have become clear that for me the result was wholly negative. I could not get at the meaning of what I was seeing with the help of what I knew in India, though it is possible that Englishmen will be able to feel from what I have said that their religious experience is very different from ours.

If I could not understand what they were getting from their religious observances, I was not less baffled by two other questions — how much of their religious practice went deeper than the continuation of a respected tradition and how much faith was still left among them? Of course, I saw that a new cathedral was being built even in this age. That was at Guildford. It had arisen on a commanding site, and the main structure with the nave and aisles had been completed. Only the apse still remained to be built. There was a good deal of the spirit of the Middle Ages in the manner in which it was being built. Did that indicate the presence of a living faith, or was it only a continuation of the forms of the old civilization?

Even on the assumption that it was nothing more, it would be evidence in favour of the conclusion that religion and civilization were still interwoven with each other in England, as indeed in the West as a whole. What I saw gave me an even stronger feeling. It seemed to me that as soon as the life of the English people lost touch with religion it also passed beyond the pale of civilization to that *de-civilized* state created for a very large number of the people of the West by industrialism and democracy.

An incident at Canterbury made me aware of this. A party of visitors, clearly English, was being taken round the Cathedral by a clergyman. In the very church of Thomas à Becket he was having to explain to them who Thomas was, and yet just in front of them I saw the steps which had been worn down by the pilgrims who had gone up in double rows on their knees to the shrine. These men and women had even to be told who the Black Prince was. I, who had learned about both in a jungle of East Bengal before I was twelve, was deeply shocked in my historical consciousness. I asked some of my English friends in dismay whether knowledge of history was disappearing among them. They said that there was a good deal of ignorance of even the elementary facts of English history. Afterwards I realized that it was not a question of that alone. They had lost touch with religion, and had never trodden the Pilgrims' Way. They were falling from the civilized state for having acquired, not forbidden knowledge, but forbidden ignorance.

I do not think that there is any pretence of secularity in any aspect of the civilization of the English people. When in one of my writings I referred to the Coronation as a *secular* ritual, an English friend asked me in surprise why I had used *that* adjective. Even their deepest and highest scientific thought would not have been what it is except for that deep brooding over the mystery of existence which religion alone has fostered so far. In saying this I am not thinking simply of Newton, or Faraday, but even of Rutherford, Jeans, and Thomson. Even if all that could be forgotten, there would still remain the *mores* of the whole people, which are infused with the spirit that Christianity has created.

It is felt instanteously in the reverence which accompanies their religious rituals. I noticed this in the behaviour of the choir boys in King's College Chapel. As they went about placing the music and books on the stands, they looked like young priests. When they sang they appeared angelic, so that I wanted to say as Gregory the Great had done, 'Not Angles, but angles.' When I said something like that to the young lady who was showing me round Cambridge she remarked, 'Some of them are little devils, though.' I could well believe that. But that was what most forcibly demonstrated the influence of religion on them. It was symbolic of the transformation of those wild folks from the German forests and Scandinavian fjords into civilized peoples.

With all this I also found a sociological fact in connection with religion, in which England to my thinking presented a complete contrast to India. There the so-called upper classes were more religious than the common people, while in India the situation is exactly the opposite. Religion belongs to the people, and the upper classes boast of their irreligiosity. It is not simply that they have lost a particular faith. Men are always doing so, and without that there can be no spiritual progress. But men are also striving after and sometimes finding new faiths. The upper classes in India are losing, and have largely lost, their capacity for faith, and they no longer feel its need. As an accident of history has for the time being made them the most prosperous section of the people of India in the worldly sense, they do not see the unhappiness of their state.

PART IV
State Of The Nation

I

A Constitutional Parliament

In beginning this part of the book, in which I wish to set down what little I have to say about the contemporary situation of the English people, I am reminded of the tale of the third calender in *The Arabian Nights*. That is the story of the prince who spent a delightful year in the company of forty princesses and then, when they had gone to pay a visit to their father, came to grief by opening a door which they had implored him in tears not to open. I have wondered why the girls, when they were so afraid of the risk, did not take the obvious precaution of carrying away the key with them. But, of course, the story-teller made them give it to the prince, because for once an Oriental wished to demonstrate that, besides Fate, man's perverse will and fallible nature also could bring about his ruin and degradation. So the prince duly succumbed to the temptation, and opening the door came upon a beautiful horse in the hall beyond. As he was a lover of fine horses he took it out to ride. But the animal was a winged horse, and as soon as the prince mounted its back it spread out two mighty wings and flew away, ultimately throwing him down and blinding one of his eyes by pricking it with the tip of a wing. I am afraid that by trying to write about the present state of the English people I am courting a similar fate. But why am I taking the risk at all?

In my broadcasts I had to include the subject because the B.B.C. expected me to say something about the Welfare State and similar recent developments in a series of talks meant for its overseas listeners. Now, however, I am free, and there is no temptation before me, for of all the things I saw in England, contemporary conditions were those which interested me least. Indeed, more than once, I thought of omitting the topic altogether from this book. But after considering the matter further I find that there are one or two reasons which call for its inclusion.

For one thing, I saw certain aspects of the present-day life of the English people for which I was not prepared by what I had read. Perhaps they were implicit in the printed word, but some had not been fully brought home to me, and some I had simply not believed. I found the discoveries quite interesting in themselves, and others might like to hear about them.

Moreover, I think I ought to cover the present situation to give completeness to my account. Not that I am afraid of being criticized for being taken up exclusively with the traditional aspects of English life and civilization. These are, to my thinking, the only ones that deserve attention in their own right. Nevertheless, I also think that the Timeless England whose presence I felt so strongly and which I have described in my own way, will remain hanging in the air and may even be dismissed as a fantasy of my own imagination unless I bring it in relation with present-day conditions.

I became aware of this risk when soon after my return I went to speak before a very intelligent audience of students in Delhi on the cultural life of the English people. At the end of my talk a young man, possibly a disciple of one of the disciples of the London School of Economics, got up and observed that I seemed to have a very narrow notion of culture, for I had not said a word about the Welfare State and economic questions, which were surely as much a part of culture as literature, art, the stage and the other things I had described.

The objection was so unexpected that I had no answer to it, and simply replied that I had spoken according to my lights, old lights, wax-lights in the days of electricity, so to speak. But I have now recovered my wits, and have arrived at a view of the connection between the Welfare State and other contemporary phenomena on the one hand and the traditional features of English civilization on the other, which will give greater solidity to my description of them and vindicate my stand. This view will come out gradually in the course of what follows. But in the first instance I shall give an account of my discoveries, beginning with politics.

Until very recently, before the people of the West began to

admire us as promising parliamentarians, with even otherwise sensible Englishmen joining in the chorus to gain some private end, England was the Mecca of politically-minded Indians, and the House of Commons the stone of Kaaba. Since I belong to one of these older generations I should have been keen on seeing something of English political life. But for a number of reasons I had come to lose interest in it, and was not willing to devote any considerable time out of my all-too-short stay to something which had no great appeal for me. Nevertheless, I was bound to be shown a little of it, and I am glad of that, because even that superficial view gave me clues to the course of English politics since the end of the war, by which I had been very much puzzled.

It began with a visit to the House of Commons, and the experience was memorable in its way. The chamber itself was fine, and I thought that it had been rebuilt with impeccable taste and propriety. There was a good deal of very becoming architectural piety in it. But what was happening within affected me very peculiarly. I could not bring myself to believe that what I was seeing and hearing was in any way connected with government, or with the cruel trade of politics, in which good-nature had no place. On the contrary, the mental state created within me by the proceedings was a more or less close anticipation of what I felt at Sadler's Wells the same night, and at the Horse Guards a few days later, when I went to see the ceremony of Changing the Guard.

Curiously enough, it was the greatest Parliamentarian of our times, Sir Winston Churchill, whom I regard also as the greatest political figure of our age and perhaps the greatest the world has seen since Napoleon, Bismarck, and Lincoln, who contributed most to this impression. I saw him in what may have been his last appearance as Prime Minister in the House, and I was astonished by his wholly unstatesmanlike appearance and behaviour. He was not there when the sitting began, but came in unobserved by me while I was listening to an exchange between a Minister and a Labour front-bencher. Suddenly, turning my eyes to another part of the Treasury Bench, I saw an old gentleman huddled up between two colleagues. It was Churchill, whose portrait hung in my study during the war by the side of a large reproduction of the *Mona Lisa*, to the scandal and indignation of my cultured and patriotic friends.

He looked very much like his figure in a toby jug, but was much more rosy, white-haired, and childlike than I could have imagined him to be. It was surprising how successfully he had divested himself of all atmosphere, of all suggestion of being not only a writer, historian and political thinker, but also a statesman and war leader. He showed no signs of being weighed down with anxiety for anything, the world or his country, war or peace. He had no brooding prophetic air, no eagle glances, no rebukes for anybody. He appeared like a schoolboy in a class of schoolboys, not like a teacher among school children, as our new statesmen in India always try to look. Winston Churchill the statesman and Winston Churchill the House of Commons man seemed to be wholly different persons.

I cannot say either that the others created a different and more political impression. Everybody in that chamber seemed to be conforming to some pre-established pattern of behaviour, a fixed code which laid down that the debates should have an air of high-spirited and even angry contests and yet mean nothing at all in the upshot. The questions and answers seemed to me to be more like the pulling of crackers by two friends than the sharp rapier thrusts they were meant to resemble. I asked myself, ' What is the meaning of this highly stylized behaviour?' As the question rose in my mind, the answer also suggested itself.

What I was seeing was a traditional and even venerable ritual, which had to be gone through correctly, decorously, and even in a devout manner, in order to maintain the tradition of parliamentary government. Of course, I could also feel that there was a practical purpose behind this ritual, but that was a purpose which was contained within the four corners of the new role of the House of Commons. It seemed that after establishing a constitutional monarchy the English people had taken another great step in the evolution of their political institutions by bringing into existence a purely constitutional form of parliamentary government, in which the House of Commons also reigned but did not govern, that business having passed to one of the parties chosen by the people and entrusted with power for the time being.

This, however, is no triumph for the caucus or a fulfilment of the old saying that the best party is but a conspiracy against the rest of the nation. For if there is any conspiracy in party rule, the whole nation has fully entered into it. It makes use of the party system to run the government according to its wishes and to keep the bureaucracy, if not quite under its thumb, at all events in reins. Through the same system the nation keeps the ruling party subservient, for it can always turn that party out.

In this system of government, which can be described as a plebiscitary oligarchy, Parliament definitely has its place, because the party chosen by the people cannot take over the government and administration directly, but has in the first instance to hold a majority in the House of Commons, and also because the House still remains the most important platform from which to canvass the people for the next lease of power. It is, however, a formal constitutional role. As to real government, the party in power can do anything it likes, so long as it keeps the nation pleased.

If there is anything at all in this view of the role of the House of Commons today, then it is pointless to complain that it is composed of small men. What business can bigness have in it, even when present in individual members? The formal duty of an M.P. is to keep the conventions and appearance of parliamentary government going. His real duty is to serve the party, passively in any case by always voting for it, and actively, if he has the brains for it, by making persuasive speeches to convince the people that the rule of the party is also the rule of reason and justice, for even though true democracy is government by collective whim, no electorate likes to think that it is being whimsical. In addition, the members have an overriding duty to themselves, which is to remain members, and some also think that in fairness to themselves they cannot turn a blind eye to the prospect of becoming a Minister.

None of these functions of an M.P. calls for greatness in the usually understood sense of the word. Voting for the party is a fundamental duty for him, but it has no connection with ability. Edward Gibbon, an undoubted genius in his line, made no bones about it. He said, 'I took my seat at the beginning of the memorable contest between Great Britain and America, and supported, with many a sincere and silent vote, the rights, though not, perhaps, the interests of the mother-country.' Today the party demands the silent vote, whether it is sincere or not, with even greater insistence than in the past, and the member does not expect a sinecure.

The other functions of an M.P., particularly that of becoming a minister, require certain kinds of ability. As Thomas Jefferson has said: 'If due participation of office is a matter of right, how are vacancies to be obtained? Those by death are few, by resignation none.' In India the insistence on the right is so great that a Chief Minister has to create *ad hoc* vacancies to satisfy it. In England this cannot be done, and therefore ability even now has some place in Parliament. But it can be a specialized kind of ability, and sometimes only of the kind which in the days of William Pitt the Elder made the Duke of Newcastle, and not him, the first man in Parliament.

Thus whether there will be greatness in or about Parliament depends wholly on external circumstances. The safe rule is to assume that if the English people are themselves doing big things in politics, some greatness will also make its appearance in Parliament. If they are not, any greatness that any member might possess will remain unutilized and unperceived. In a word, the greatness of the House of Commons can only be a reflected greatness. The two World Wars with the two periods of peace following them have proved that decisively enough. In a peace-time Parliament a natural selection operates against a Lloyd George or a Churchill.

FAREWELL TO POLITICS

THE QUESTION TO ASK in connection with the current politics of the English people is not whether the House of Commons is composed of small men, but whether the nation itself is interested in doing great things in politics. I do not think so. The English have lost, not only their political ambitions, but also the greater part of their zest in politics. The only people who seem to be capable of working themselves up to a state of excitement over politics are the politicians themselves, whose personal and party interests are involved. That was the impression I got in England, which confirmed what I had vaguely felt before, and all that I have been reading since then has been confirming the impression itself.

Political interest, power, and passion are not things which have to be discovered by statistical analysis. If they are present they also make themselves felt in a highly wrought-up psychological state. I observed this for over forty years in my country, when the nationalist movement had set itself to secure our independence. Even when there is no subjection to foreign rule, the impact of live politics is felt as the current is felt in a river. English politics gave me the feeling that I was watching a swimming pool.

I was in England on the eve of a general election, and heard a political debate between two front-rank politicians, one Labour and the other Conservative. The formal announcement of the coming election had not been made as yet, so the Conservative spokesman could not say anything about it. The Labour politician took it as a certainty, and spoke bravely about questions from the audience, and my friend from the B.B.C. said that it was a very good discussion. I could not help saying to myself, 'What a queer idea they have of a good political debate!'

The election campaign was even more unimpressive. I left England just as it was getting into its stride, and so I did not see its real form. But even the little I saw and heard was enough to show that it was a very tame affair. One day, at a party, a Conservative member of Parliament told me when I asked him about the possible result that his party would win by fifty-four seats. If he could get so close to the final result before any polling had taken place, the election could not even have been as exciting as a friendly game of cricket, let alone a Test Match. Altogether, it seemed to have very little significance.

Of course, since the attainment of independence, which the English people describe as their *gift* to us, and which we look upon as our *victory* over them, there has visibly been a marked decline of political interest even in India, compared with what could be seen before. But there is still sufficient factional rivalry to make the elections lively. There is also suffering and discontent enough to make it necessary for a government which calls itself parliamentary democracy to have recourse to shooting and gassing as a matter of regular administrative routine more often than in any other independent country in the contemporary world. All this keeps the spirit of politics alive. But can Englishmen imagine that in any circumstances they would hear the sound of rifle fire or bursting tear-gas bombs in their streets, or see buses and tramcars set on fire? I suppose they would sooner expect a volcano to erupt in the heart of London. Therefore, quite naturally, they look upon the speakers in Hyde Park as typical demagogues. That alone indicates what liveliness is left in English politics.

It must not be imagined, however, that I am saying this in a spirit of criticism or condemnation. If the English people are no longer able to get excited over politics it is because they have solved all their political problems or got rid of them, and so there is nothing left for them to do. At home they have ended social and economic injustice, so far as this can be removed at all in human society, and thus deprived their politics of its most powerful motive force. They have also eliminated all competition for political power by distributing it among all, and making it diffuse to the point of ineffectiveness. It is hardly likely that any class or any tyrant will arise among them in the future to monopolize political power and create a new struggle for it.

The only domestic problem they have still on their hands is not a political problem at all, though successive Governments are being saddled with it. It is the problem of living like a nation of gentlemen without the means of a gentleman on the national scale. It is a problem for the nation as a whole to solve, or it has to find its own solution. Any mere Government can deal with it only by adroit accounting, which is no cure at all but only a palliative. But since the English people will not face up to it — no elderly gentleman who is in financial embarrassment ever does — Governments, like the estate managers of *grands seigneurs,* are having to make a pretence of dealing with it.

If this is the state of politics at home, there is even less to do in the outside world. I have never read about any people who have been so happy to lose an empire and so ready to think that the loss is really a great gain. That simply shows that in spite of having created the greatest empire that history has seen, the English people never had any real understanding of empires. Those who have do not lose them in less than two hundred years. Consider the Russians, for instance. They and the English started their respective imperial enterprises at about the same epoch. But while the British Empire has disappeared, the Russian is still going strong, and despite the gabble and din about ending European colonialism, not one man in Asia raises his voice for the liberation of the largest number of Asiatics still under White rule. The truth is that only dying empires are kicked, living one never.

In the field of international politics, too, the English people are clearly conscious of the limits of their power, though they are not quite as frank about that as they are about the Empire. Taken all in all, then, what they want today in the way of politics is not politics properly so-called, but only *administration,* with a little politics to keep the bureaucracy in check. In such circumstances why should they be excited over politics?

On the other hand, it would seem that the only thing which can still rouse political passion and even fury among the English people is any attempt at involving them again in real politics. That was seen during the Suez affair. Memories of political power and action do not die out in a day, and Sir Anthony Eden and his supporters may have been carried away by them in a momentary throw-back to the past. But a cry of horror went up from at least half the nation. The mood of political holiness which had been sedulously developed in England to hide the absence of political power was shocked when a British Government suddenly showed signs of reverting to the unregenerate state by trying to partake once more of the fleshpots of Egypt. Yet it must be admitted that there was a hard core of common sense in the outcry, hysterical and sanctimonious as it was. The old prerogative of bombarding Copenhagen or Alexandria could simply not be exercised in the changed circumstances of the English people.

But I cannot see any vestige of sense in the behaviour of those other Englishmen who cannot forget their political past and who think they are continuing it by practising a peculiarly self-deluding form of pseudo-politics, based mainly on clichés. Catchwords have always been the camp-followers of politics, but in many parts of the world today they are all that is left of it. So it is in England, and this I cannot understand, for in the past the hardest thinking in politics has always been seen when a nation has been in the midst of its worst troubles. Think of Plato, Aristotle, Cicero, St Augustine, Machiavelli, Hobbes, or Burke. They came to be regarded as political thinkers by rising above catchwords, but in the contemporary world the only sure means of being hailed as a saviour of nations is to dole out nothing but cant. Emotionally, also, the English people have developed a very peculiar yearning:

> To hear the world applaud the hollow ghost
> Which blamed the living man.

This is not a political book, and I will leave it at that. But I hope the English people will understand the hint, if their preference for understatement still holds good for politics.

I am glad to be able to say that the great majority of Englishmen are not of this way of thinking. They are too insular for that, and the Englishman is at his strongest and best when he is most insular. Even in olden days this made a thoroughgoing English imperialist a man of two minds, and the Little-

Englander trait has won. It appears to me that the English people have reached a stage in their national evolution when they would be only too happy to say like the Duke in *As You Like It*:

> *Now, my co-mates and brothers in exile,*
> *Hath not old custom made this life more sweet*
> *Than that of painted pomp? Are not these woods*
> *More free from peril than the envious court?*
>
>   .   .   .   .   .
>
> *And this our life* exempt *from* public haunt
> *Finds tongues in trees, books in the running brooks,*
> *Sermons in stones, and good in every thing.*
> *I would not change it.*

And I would say:

> *Happy is your grace,*
> *That can translate the stubbornness of fortune*
> *Into so quiet and so sweet a style.*

But no, because non-political idylls are impossible of realization. The unpleasant truth is that even if a nation wants to give up politics, politics will not give it up. When Greek politics came to an end the Romans stepped in. When we Hindus lost or sterilized our politics the Muslims conquered us. And when the Muslims themselves were exhausted the Europeans marched in to fill the vacuum. The only sure means of doing away with politics is not to allow it to survive in any part of the world. I hope one day a worldwide political tyranny will make non-political private citizens of us all. But since that is not likely to happen in any predictable future, the yearning for a non-political existence finds expression in a different manner. All the tailless foxes of the world are appealing to the only two with brushes still left — and these the finest ever seen in the world — to cut them off. But the eloquence has not borne any fruit, nor ever will, it would seem.

This is bringing about a strange contradiction in the life of all peoples who are tired of politics and want to live in peace. For instance, there is nothing from which the English people shrink with greater horror than the mere idea of war, yet they are having to spend more money on armaments than at any other time in their long and warlike history. They denounce the H-bomb every day and still cannot refrain from making it. They are determined not to go to war, and yet they allow a foreign nation to have military bases on their own soil. All this is done in the name of practical politics. But if idealistic politics and practical politics have parted company in this fashion there cannot be any sense in either.

I myself was startled by what I saw of military preparations in the peaceful English scene. Both at Cambridge and Oxford I heard the screams of jets in the sky. To hear that sound in the eternal silence of those infinite spaces, and in a country which on the ground has absorbed a good deal of that stillness, was terrifying. I cannot tell how much I disliked the immense American airfield which I saw when going from Cambridge to Ely. From the tower of the cathedral I saw the winding Ouse below, and the trails of the jets above.

All this is bringing a futile, and not ennobling, tragedy into the life of the English people. What a fine thing their farewell to politics would have been without it!

III

THE WELFARE STATE—FACT OR HOAX?

As AGAINST DEAD OR dying English politics it was a genuine surprise and pleasure to find that the Welfare State was a reality. I had not expected that at all. Almost all that I had read about it had sounded like election speeches, and unfortunately the phrase has been used as a party cry. Besides, whenever I find that a political or economic formula has been taken over from the West by our politicians I become suspicious of it, and the discredit into which it falls is reflected on the original. So I did not go to England with any faith in the Welfare State, far less with any ready-made admiration for it. But after seeing it with my own eyes I came away with a genuine respect for it.

I hope, however, that the thing for which I acquired this respect the same as that which is called the Welfare State in England. This may or may not be the case, for the term has never been very clearly defined. Those who speak about it most often are politicians, who prefer ambiguity as an aid to deception, and deception is of the very essence of politics. The man who described religion as the opium of the people never tried to define what kind of dope political and economic dogmas were, because he was interested in the popularization of a particular drug of his own. At best politics makes use of lies as a thin film of lubricant on its bearings, at worst it is all lubricant. The great majority of the peoples of the world are, unfortunately, used to the lubricant alone.

However that might be, when I speak of the Welfare State I understand two things: first, a government which is trying to promote the welfare of the people and making contributions to it; secondly, a general state of welfare of the people, which may or may not be due to the government and its agencies. I saw both kinds of welfare in England, and shall set down my impressions about them, without attempting to determine how they are inter-related. I am unable to do that.

To see the government and the public bodies connected with it making a contribution to the welfare of the people in actual fact, and not simply claiming to do so as a matter of political propaganda, gave me a strange sensation. In the first place, it was something to come upon a government at all disposed to give value for the money it was taking from the people by taxation. In India, more than anywhere else in the world, the money that we give to Caesar is regarded as Caesar's, and as the bribe to keep him from taking more. If anybody says that this is not the view of taxation among the masses of India even today, he simply does not know India, and I had come from India.

But the main reason for the sensation of strangeness I had was that I was used to the old personal method of dealing with all the problems of living, including funerals. When a man is used to seeing these solved only by the individual's own efforts or not at all, he is bound to be struck by the unnaturalness of finding them taken out of his hands, if not wholly, at least partially. Yet this unnatural state of affairs exists in England.

If anything convinced me of the reality of the Welfare State more than anything else, it was the National Health Service. In India it is not semi-starvation, to which most of us are inured, but illness that sets the most harrowing personal problems. Good treatment is expensive, and free treatment in the public hospitals most often casual and unsympathetic, and not infrequently humiliating as well. I had no need for medical attention in England, but I know the case of a young countryman of mine who was only passing through the country on his way to the United States. He went to a hospital for a check, and it was discovered that he had a touch of tuberculosis. So he was kept and treated in a hospital for some months, to the incredulous relief of his family and himself. In India tuberculosis is either a catastrophe for the family or slow death for the patient. But so short are the memories of men that the people of England have learnt to complain bitterly if they have to spend even five pounds on treatment.

The building effort was the second thing which made me admit the existence of the Welfare State. What has been done in England may not be enough to meet all the needs, but I had never seen anything like that before and would not have believed that so much had been done unless I had seen some of it myself. I wondered why I had heard so little about this building activity. In our country so much is said as soon as some scheme appears on paper that people do not notice anything when a project is finished, nor do they blame anybody if it is not.

The phrase 'English slums' is still symbolic of the condition of working men in England with most of us. Before I left India a friend asked me to make a point of seeing them, perhaps thinking that the experience would cure me of the chronic Anglomania with which they all think I am afflicted. I cannot say that in certain parts of London, Birmingham, and Bristol I did not see what are called slums in England, but they did not agree with my conception of them, which was formed from the slums of Calcutta and Delhi, of which I knew a great deal. On the contrary, the new blocks of flats for working men had the appearance of the blocks of luxury flats in New Delhi, in those parts of this upstart city which since Independence we have got into the habit of calling 'prestige areas' because foreigners, diplomats, and people of similar status live there. Even in those parts of the East End of London where the old working men's dwellings had survived, as for instance in Bethnal Green, I saw prams at the doors, and curtains in the windows, which instead of suggesting slums suggested to me the quarters of high civil servants of the Government of India.

One day I was taken to County Hall where I had a long conversation with a woman architect and town-planner of the L.C.C. I asked her about her work, and she replied that her assignment was Lansbury in the Poplar Community, which covered an area of about 124 acres, and would eventually house some 9,500 people, or about 42 per cent of the pre-war population.

It is a question of rebuilding then?

Not quite, she explained, for they were trying really to reshape the area and make the people who would come into it live a different kind of life. To begin with, the scattered industries were to be grouped into an industrial zone. Then blocks of flats were to be built, and after that markets and shops, schools, churches, and other public buildings. Of course, these meant not only more amenities for the inhabitants, but also a different kind of life.

Had anything been completed?

Yes, the first stage. Blocks of flats, maisonnettes, and terrace houses for about 1,500 people had been completed. There were besides a shopping centre, a market-place, three schools, a number of churches, with a home for the aged, three public houses, three children's playgrounds, and a small amenity park.

She showed me a large model, on which the completed portions and those to be built were differently coloured. 'It does not look like an industrial area, though,' I remarked.

'Perhaps not,' she replied, 'for we have adopted a new layout, which is different from the old. The main idea is to have a series of neighbourly groups linked together by open spaces. In fact, the open spaces form a special feature of the rebuilding. We are also giving the buildings different heights to avoid monotony; the open spaces are of different sizes too. Altogether, we want to give an air of spaciousness and variety to the area. We have nevertheless used the bricks and purple-grey slates which are traditional in this part of London.'

That ended the conversation, and I left. But I am very suspicious of models and plans, so I went down to see what the place really looked like, and I found the rebuilt area exactly as it was in the model. In Birmingham and Bristol, too, I saw a good deal of this type of rebuilding.

I shall not try to list all the aspects of the state's welfare activities, but pass on to the appearance of welfare in the people. It was so decisive that even what was on the surface gave to me, who had come from India, an impression of extravagant luxury. The first effect of this is bedazzlement. Some try to recover from it by recalling the East's spiritual superiority over the materialistic West, others call nationalism to the rescue and try to convince themselves that all this luxury has been made possible by the economic exploitation of the East. But in the end the facts produce their effect, and most Eastern visitors feel glad that there is so much welfare going, more especially because in the Welfare State there is hardly any distinction made between the natives and the foreigners.

But it would still be possible for us Indians to go wrong over the meaning of all the abundance and luxury that is to be seen in England. India is a country of very great disparities of wealth, perhaps the greatest disparities existing in the present-day world. In our country there can be no comparison even between the ways of living of a middle-class family of average means and a well-to-do family. The two stand at wholly different levels of material culture, as anthropologists say. The peasant and the artisan in the villages live below the standard of livestock in England.

So an Indian might imagine that the abundance was only for a minority living in ease on the exploitation of the majority, unless he took the trouble of looking closer at the life of the people at large, which would show that want and distress had disappeared from it. In India both lie on the surface, and no one can avoid noticing them. They are obvious in the first instance in the clothing. Even in the big cities, for every two persons in clean and adequate clothing there are eight in an assortment of shabby, dirty, insufficient, and tattered clothes. In the cold season, as I travel in the public transport of Delhi, I often have sitting by my side men who have wrapped themselves with dirty blankets or quilts in which to all appearance they have been sleeping for years. In the villages it is virtually impossible to meet men in clean and adequate clothing.

After that the most painful impression is created by the presence of diseased, underfed and deformed persons everywhere. Again, almost every day in the buses I have to sit by the side of people suffering from all kinds of illness, including tuberculosis and chickenpox. The unfortunate lepers are everywhere. Even when there is no disease the impression is one of lifelessness.

To see this day after day for years in all public places creates a mental distress from which it is impossible to escape even in one's home. This mental suffering becomes almost physical pain when the children are seen to be in the same state, and except for the Punjabi children all children in India fare worse' than the grown-ups. Upper-class Indians who cannot stomach this universal exhibition of squalor and distress run away from their people to live an artificially protected life in carefully segregated places like New Delhi, do not go about except in cars, and never visit the so-called 'city', where ordinary Indians live. And in India the helpers of people in distress are always people in slightly less distress.

The absence of all this in England made me believe in the Welfare State. Especially, it was a joy to see the children. I have heard even Englishmen say that when they see the new generations of children they do not grumble at the taxation. I could never distinguish between the children of the different social classes, though in my country I can place them within twenty-five rupees of the income of their parents. Whether they were playing in the Victoria Park in Bethnal Green or riding in Rotten Row, all seemed alike to my inexperienced eyes. During my stay in England, in the course of which I saw hundreds of children, I saw only one in insufficient clothing. That was in an industrial quarter of Birmingham. The boy was in a shirt and shorts only, and his feet were bare. I do not know why he was dressed like that, but he seemed healthy, and he looked back and grinned at me again and again when he saw that I was noticing him.

I do not know, however, why I should have to collect evidence and set it forth to prove the state of well-being of the general mass of the English people. The news has reached even our masses. While highbrow Indians affect to believe that the English people are finished, humble and common folk all over the sub-continent of India are coming more and more to believe that they will no longer remain poor if only they can make their way to England. Who brings this story to them? Indian workmen and tradesmen who have been to England, of course. Before I left for England I went to do some shopping, and the owner of the shop said to me when he heard where I was going: 'Sir, you will see what the country is like. Please take your weight before you leave and again after you have returned. Compare the two.'

Another day, after my return, as I was going to New Delhi in a bus, a Sikh in very ordinary dress came and sat by me. He asked the conductor for some direction, and got no reply. Then he turned to me and said, 'See how they treat a countryman if he does not look rich. I have lived for years in London, and I have never seen anything like this.' He explained that he had a business in the East End. Then we began to discuss living expenses in England as compared with those in India. I observed that rents were very high. The Sikh at once replied, 'Why should you go on paying rent? It is so easy to buy a house there. I have bought one for five thousand pounds. I paid a part of the price down, and then had the balance spread over years.'

Such are the stories which are reaching the common people of India, and it is no wonder that hundreds and even thousands in my country and Pakistan are applying for passports. There is even some business in forged passports. If the Governments of the two countries had not been very strict about granting passports, the English people would by this time have discovered what a terrific reputation their Welfare State has built up for itself in the East. It is literally a fulfilment of the old song:

> They say they scorn to tell you lies,
> That they are not mistaken,
> But the streets are paved with pudding-pies,
> Nay, powdered beef and bacon.

> You that are free to cross the seas
> Make no more disputation;
> In Lubberland you'll at ease
> With pleasant recreation.

IV

The Most Glorious Revolution

If I HAD NOT been to England I should have continued in a wholly wrong view of the English social and economic revolution of our times. It has been represented to the outside world, so far as it has been explained at all, in a very partisan light, as the achievement of the Labour Party. We in India with our bias in favour of Labour have given it an even more flamingly partisan colour, and come to regard it as the victory of the good Englishmen led by Attlee over the wicked ones led by Churchill. In brief, to most of us the English Welfare State is the product, if not the mere by-product, of a class conflict, in which we have every right to be the *tertius gaudens*.

This is not as absurd a mistake as many Englishmen might suppose. We have no means of knowing how much of the class animus of the Labour spokesmen is only a political convention or at the worst the continuation of an emotional disposition acquired in the past but of no practical importance now. Even today some genuine Labourites have within themselves a wholly superfluous string which vibrates to the underdog leitmotif, and some spurious ones, who are mostly the maladjusted scions of the old ruling class, cannot forget their sense of grievance against their parents even though they have no real grievances left. These talking fossils are taken very seriously by us, because our slogan for a world policy is, 'Malcontents of the world, unite!'

It was only after visiting England that I realized what a mistake I was committing. Even the little I saw convinced me that the English revolution of our times was in the first instance a *national* revolution, and not the class revolution that I had imagined it to be. I found no trace of resentment against it, I mean real anger as distinct from the grumbling in all circumstances which is normal in Englishmen. There was resignation even to the heavy taxation. It was a case either of demoralization of the once-privileged classes or of co-operation on their part even at their own expense. I would not say that the English upper classes are absolutely free from the feeling that they are being hit hard and even treated unjustly, but it is equally certain that as a whole they would not like to see undone anything that has been brought about by way of equalization of incomes and national welfare.

I am sure I am not wrong in thinking that the Welfare State is a state of the English conscience rather than of the English economy. Perhaps if the English people had considered their economy dispassionately there would have been no Welfare State at all. I should have been surprised by this economic imprudence if I did not remember that the English upper classes always had a very active social conscience. If at times in the past they could not make out why those who wanted dinner did not simply ring for it, they also got into a terrific state of excitement and consciousness of sin when they found out that ringing was not enough. I do not understand why it should be forgotten that social reform in England began to come from the top long before it was demanded from below.

In saying this I have no wish to deny to the Labour Party the credit that is due to it. But in 1945 it was as nearly a national party as it is possible for any party to be. The English party system originated in factions, but it is the glory of English political life to have broken this wild horse to a beneficent purpose, to have utilized it in such a way that something which was regarded by moralists as an eternal and universal evil has become a mechanism of change and growth. Thus in matters of national policy the English people are united to a degree of which the outside world has a very imperfect idea.

The next impression that I formed was that the English revolution was not a proletarian revolution at all. Though it has made very great progress towards creating a classless, or more accurately a one-class society, it is meaningless and even absurd to call it Communistic or even Socialistic. It is not even a trade unionists' revolution, powerfully as the Trade Union movement has contributed to it. It is really a revolution which is almost a contradiction in terms—a bourgeois revolution. Or should I say that all revolutions, including the French and the Russian — the two which have come to be regarded as supremely typical — have been bourgeois revolutions and that the phrase 'proletarian revolution' is itself a contradiction in terms? Anyhow that is what has happened in England, and was bound to happen. The English people have always been so class-conscious that their egalitarianism could only be an ideal of levelling up, attended by some levelling down only because there was not enough going to build everybody country houses or confer peerages on all. I think, if they had the means, they would have done that. Since they have not, the unavoidable compromise is to make everybody middle-class. In England a new classless society is coming into existence in which most people will be able to feel class-proud.

The English revolution appeared to have a third feature of which even Englishmen seemed to be unaware. It was an industrial revolution in a new sense, because it was transforming not only economic life and organization, but also human personality and character by giving both an industrialized cast. I had no suspicion of this before I went to England, and indeed could not have, living in India. In my country the distinction between the peasant and the townsman — the agricultural and the industrial man — is as fundamental even today as the distinction between the hunter and the peasant was in the early age of agriculture. Besides, I had read so much about the English peasant that I had no inkling of the fact that he had disappeared from the English scene. I expected to meet him in the English countryside as I meet the Indian peasant in the Indian countryside. But I failed to meet Farmer Oak in Wessex. I saw many English villages which answered every previous conception I had about them, but the English peasant no longer lived in them. The village had survived architecturally, but not, so far as I could judge, socially.

This cannot seem more strange to Englishmen than it did to me. I saw agriculture and animal husbandry everywhere. Even though I had come from a country which was overwhelmingly agricultural I was astonished by the standard of English agriculture and animal husbandry. I had never seen anything like it. Ours in comparison was so very primitive and poor. But the peasant, the shepherd and the herdsman were absent. I saw hardly half a dozen people at work on the land, and I came across only three horse-drawn ploughs. Agricultural and pastoral activity appeared to be impersonal.

Then I inferred what I did not actually see. I concluded that the men and women who were engaged in tilling the land and rearing livestock in England in our age were no longer the peasant and cattle-raiser of tradition and history but had been transformed into a sort of industrial worker. This process was making a substantial contribution to the emergence of the one-class bourgeois society about which I have already written.

To me it seems very strange that the English people, who are so acutely conscious of the industrialization of their landscape, and very alarmed and aggrieved about it, should be so silent about, if not unaware of, the industrialization of personality and character. Yet I thought that the changes in the English scene were minor compared with the changes in the human beings. The encroachment of industrialism on the landscape is a sore point with all Englishmen. Perhaps I may set down my impressions about it. If I were asked how much disfigurement I noticed I would say that to my way of thinking it was not much, and even of this I should not have become aware unless I had previously read a good deal about it. It may give some comfort to Englishmen to learn that in my own lifetime I have seen greater and uglier encroachments on nature in India, which has still to industrialize herself, than all that has come about in England in two hundred years. Even waste land has been robbed of its gaunt and ascetic dignity.

Besides, I perceived a fundamental difference between the industrial landscape that was now being created in a deliberate and planned manner and that which had been brought into existence by the first uncontrolled and indisciplined onrush of the Industrial Revolution. This distinction is comparable to that which exists between the industrial worker of today and the exploited factory hands of a hundred years ago. Shortly after my arrival I saw an old and a modern factory of a well-known firm of manufacturers which made me conscious of this. Later on I observed a good deal more of this contrast.

I think the spirit of planned urbanism, about which I have already said something, is very active and it is replacing the old thoughtlessness. What I saw of contemporary industrial building gave me the impression that the industrial landscape was being lightened up, made quiet, and given restfulness. I feel sure that within a foreseeable time industrial England will no longer look like what it was even twenty years ago, and this will give a tangible, material expression to the welfare of the people, for one of the worst things about industrialism so far has been that through sheer ugliness in building it created an appearance of poverty even where there was no poverty. If industrial England is redesigned and rebuilt as it promises to be, the appearance of the country will create an impression as misleading in its way as the old industrialism did in another way — it will make people believe that there is more wealth and prosperity in England than actually exists.

But I must also say that it is too early in the day to forecast the exact appearance of the industrial landscape of the future. In England the Industrial Revolution has still a long way to go, and whatever the manner of the industrial expansion it will make further inroads on the traditional English landscape. In point of fact I was always asking myself — In what relationship will the industrial landscape stand to the traditional scene? Will the new one, in which the airfields will be as great landmarks as cathedrals were in the old, destroy its predecessor? I could not answer the question definitely, though I did hope that everything would come right. What, however, I could see at once was the inconsistency between lamenting the industrialism of the landscape and working furiously for the industrialization of society and human personality. Why do they want a *plebs urbana* to live in an Arcadia?

I shall now put down my final impression of the English social and economic revolution: It is *no* revolution at all. A great redwood tree in California has as much or as little right to call itself the child of a revolution as the social state of the English people today. No true revolution is ever accomplished without doctrinaire revolutionaries, and they have never had a place in English reform. That is enough to reveal the true character of the English revolution, whose great glory lies in being anti-revolutionary. It is the climax of their history, and it began, not even in the times of the Tudors, but farther back with the Black Death. In any case the modern English language and the English revolution are contemporaries.

V

OH, TO LIVE IN LUBBERLAND!

THE MATERIAL WELL-BEING of the people of England put me in a very happy frame of mind, and made me take a roseate view of their contemporary existence and future. If a vague memory of their economic problems on the national plane still lingered in my mind I gave no thought to them nor did I try to reconcile my firsthand sense impressions with what I had read and heard. When I had to express an opinion on their present economic state I said that I was no economist, and quite possibly my enthusiasm was groundless. But I also said that even if one society had succeeded in eliminating human misery in its most painful form, that is, want of food and clothing for the great majority of its members, that itself was a magnificent achievement. In England I could easily see that poverty in our sense of the word did not exist. It was not simply that I did not come upon the kind of poverty which has made the masses of India dead to the feeling of poverty, there was not even that poverty which has been a life-long companion to a man like me. When I said something to this effect to a friend in England he replied in the characteristic English way that certainly if a man was not very careless or lazy there was no reason for anyone in England to be half-fed or half-clad. There was no suggestion in his tone that he was speaking about a condition in human society which was unprecedented. That too was remarkable. So I thought that, whatever the future might hold in store for the English people, it was something to have this state of well-being even as an interlude of fifty or twenty-five years. All that I had read about the economic troubles of the English people became for the time being wholly unreal to me.

But the exhilaration of the first impression could not last indefinitely. When after my return to India it had worn off and I gave more thought to what I had seen, I realized that I was looking at the situation of the English people from one particular angle, that of the past in England and the present in India. I was not considering the feelings and experiences of those who were living in the Welfare State as it was. Then I saw the possibility that the Welfare State Triumphant might be totally different from the Welfare State Militant.

Even when seen in the light of the past it could be said that if the Welfare State meant great gain, some losses were also bound to come in its train. England was no more to have a Howard, Elizabeth Fry, Wilberforce or Shaftesbury; Dickens, Carlyle, Ruskin, or for that matter even the Webbs would no longer write; there would be no Chartism, Suffragette agitation, or even genuine Trade Unionism, as distinct from the championship of a vested interest, which it has become today. Still, I would say that all this would be well lost if the English people could create for their new existence ideals, aspirations, and activities as fine in their way as were the old ones in theirs. Moralists have always said that prosperity corrupts. I do not know, but I definitely know that it bores. This leads me to consider the circumstances in which, to my thinking, men can be happy in the sort of life the English people have recently created for themselves.

The very first condition of ensuring happiness in the Welfare State seems to be that it should not be stagnant, that there should always be something new to be done in it— I mean doing in the real sense, creative activity of all kinds. If I am to be frank, I would say that though the Welfare State is largely the product of compassion for ordinary folk, for the common man as the democratic cliché has it, it will be the exceptional men, those who are ready to do something in the sense I have in mind, who will ultimately justify its existence. For individuals, as for nations, doing well in life and doing something in life are contradictory aims. The real test for the Welfare State will be whether it has been able to merge the two ends, so far as they can be merged.

But it seems to me that this very important condition for the Welfare State's success is difficult of fulfilment in contemporary England. This difficulty is not due to the absence of men with a will to do something. The real trouble is that there is very little to do, and it is hard to arrive at a clear perception of what to do. On this point, ever since the end of the war, I have had a feeling that the English people are in the closing stages of one cycle of their existence and have not as yet entered on another. In fact, I said this in so many words as far back as December 1946 in an article published in *The New English Review*. This is what I wrote:

> 'Although Labour itself is working under the joyous belief that its ideas are the ideas of tomorrow, an outside observer gets the impression of seeing the past reversed in a mirror. The Labour administration is going to close an era, not open a new one.
>
> 'In due course the Leftist movement will have burnt out the legacy of Fascism and in Britain levelled up in addition the swamps left undrained in the interwar period. Then a great void is bound to be felt. Perhaps it is being felt even now, as the aftermath of the war is throwing up one harassing problem after another, and it is being discovered that there is no specifically Leftist answer to them.'

It was not the English people alone who were in this predicament, it was the same with almost all mankind. As I said in the same article:

> 'Even if the future were not generally unpredictable and relentlessly ironical of those who violate its mystery, we live at a juncture of history when it is inscrutably baffling. The very foreground is occupied by the uncertainties generated by a devastating war, which call more for an alert asepsis than quack remedies. But, puzzling as the aftermath of the war is, it is nothing compared to the fundamental uncertainty of the general human situation today. Mankind is at the initial stage of a revolution in its way of living to which probably even the introduction of agriculture furnishes no parallel....

'Man's utilization of power outside his body began with the denomination nearest his own, that of animals. It has gone forward to that which is most alien to him, mechanical cosmic power. Yet we are nowhere near the term....We do not know and cannot even now foresee what effect it will have on man's social organization, on his habits of thought, even on his physical organism and on the material resources of the earth on which it is operating. Everything is fluid.'

That was what I wrote in 1946, and the situation has not changed. So even with the best of wills what could be done?

It seems to me that the second condition of living happily in the Welfare State is equally impossible to fulfil. It is the condition that once the great majority of men in a particular society have had enough to eat they should do nothing, and only sit down and doze like cattle and sheep on their pastures. But man has left the wisdom, sanity, and the impeccable moral behaviour of the beasts far behind. Once he is relieved of anxiety in regard to survival the democratic common man will make mischief in small magnitudes but on so universal a scale that he will become more dangerous than a Chenghiz Khan or a Hitler.

There is no prank a bored human being will not play. He or she will gamble, run after other people's wives and husbands, read crime stories, dabble in sex psychology, be caddish or rowdy—all just for the sake of being uncommon. Such behaviour does not pass wholly unnoticed, but it is not considered as unnatural as it would have been among livestock.

It would seem that the Welfare State of our times has arrived too late for both of its purposes, that is to say, to be put to the best use as a means to an end, and also to be enjoyed as an end in itself. It is belated also in another very important way. It has come with the triumph of modern democracy, when the theorists and practitioners of this democracy are trying hard, out of mistaken and even undesirable idealism, to supplement political and economic equality with the equality of the mind. Now, it is a good thing to do away with the caste system by birth, also by wealth, but a deadly mistake to tamper with the natural caste system of the mind. There is nothing men resent more than to be raised above themselves against their will, which means the same thing as beyond their capacity. If I might put it that way as a Hindu, the eternal Sudras prefer to remain eternal Sudras, a very good state to be in if the Sudra is left to himself. It is curious that Europeans who are so enthusiastic over Negro and all primitive art should forget that. True Sudrahood is the lowest common denominator of a dignified and happy human state, to which at times I feel I should like to glide down instead of wearying myself by trying always to fly like Icarus, son of Daedalus.

But modern democracy is making it impossible for the good Sudra to remain a good Sudra by giving him its characteristic training and education. It has already destroyed his folk-civilization in many countries, and made a half-caste of him. In revenge the new Sudra is bringing down everybody else to his level, and he has the power to do so, for the same democracy has made him the ruler of the other castes. Thus the very democratic sentiment which has made the Welfare State possible is also contributing to its failure.

But it must be understood that I am not charging the new democracy with great vices. As a class, it has become incapable of great crimes, and even its naughtiness is trivial and vicarious. On the contrary, if I am to judge by the tone of its serious literature, it seems to be remarkably virtuous and proper in its aspirations and sentiments. But as I wrote as a young man: 'Detractors of humanity are wrong. Idealists are equally so. The average man is neither so good nor so bad as we take him to be. But this mediocrity is so terribly hard to endure.'

I am not surprised, therefore, to find that some English intellectuals are already revolting against the Welfare State, of which generally speaking the English people are so proud and as it seems to me justly proud. It is contributing its share of discontent, supplementing the quota from political frustration and economic anxiety. Perhaps more rebellion is in the offing. But the worst part of this suffering is that it is so drab. Even in writing about the present state of the English people I have caught its contagion. I am afraid this part of the book has been very dull, and boringly argumentative. I would only plead in defence that the fault is not wholly mine, a part of it is in the subject.

VI

For St George And Civilization

So the english people have to look for something on which they can fall back from their present condition: something solid and inexhaustible as a source of happiness, and proof against decay and corruption; something about which they can say that nobody is going to take it away from them. But in their entire previous history they have never had to consider such a problem. They have been getting on and succeeding for centuries, and if they had temporary setbacks they never accepted defeat, nor even admitted its possibility, but dealt with each crisis as it arose, or even merely held on, confident that they would come, or at least muddle, through.

The success of this attitude in the past has made it the standard form of English behaviour and outlook in times of trouble, and I do not think that they have lost faith in it even now. Certainly, they would not admit in a conscious argument that their present difficulties and disappointments are basically different from those of the past and that a new attitude is called for. They give the appearance of thinking that they will come through if only they can hold on like Captain MacWhirr in Conrad's *Typhoon*. (It is curious that it is a Pole, and not an Englishman, who has translated the national attitude into a personal story.) But while I see all this I also have a feeling — it is no more than that — that the problem of finding an ultimate resource has already engaged their emotional yearnings. But where can they find it?

Different peoples have different ways of finding consolation and compensation for national troubles. The Germans in the nineteenth century took refuge in scholarship and philosophy, and since the Second World War they seem to be trying to forget defeat and partition in the pursuit of money, nationally as well as individually. The first of these expedients has no appeal for the English people, and the second is out of their reach. Their Government will not allow them to forget the worries of their public existence in private prosperity.

Nor can they fall back on the creations of contemporary culture. If these could provide any comfort their creators and purveyors would have been the happiest men in England, instead of being the most discontented, peevish, and dispirited. I have a notion that in England, as indeed over the whole West, contemporary culture is a satellite thrown out by the historic civilization, and it is only moving round and round its planet. If this satellite is not wholly dead like the moon it is only because there are still a sufficient number of men in it who are continuing the cultural traditions of the original civilization and carrying on the old type of activities. As regards the strictly contemporary and new manifestation of this culture, the little that I have seen of it has enabled me to understand the feelings of Laika the dog in Sputnik II.

I shall set down my feelings about it even at the risk of being laughed to scorn by the contemporary *culturewallahs*, as I would call them in my language. They have cleverness, virtuosity, self-confidence, dogmatism; they also have almost inexhaustible arguments to deceive others and themselves; but they know as well as anybody else, particularly their victims, that they have no power to make either themselves or others happy. Theirs is a world without enjoyment. I am choked by their fiction, which at best is incompetent sociology, and by their sculpture and painting, which I cannot characterize. I went up to the door of their *sanctum sanctorum*, the Musée National d' Art Moderne in Paris, and felt so frightened that I did not pass the door: I am repelled by their anger which is querulousness, and above all by their compassion which is self-pity. Their expectations from society at large and their obsession with status are not less exasperating. Who gave Michelangelo, Dr Johnson, or Beethoven his status? And does it matter? Thus I can understand why ordinary people, who have a sure instinct for happiness, shun their work like poison, even preferring the sloppy democratic literature. They are still too honest to find pleasure in pretended enjoyment.

To be candid, there are only two fields, two connected fields, in which the human mind is still live and creative, which can provide occupation for it and give to those who can remain wholly within their limits either exultation or in any case a happy forgetfulness of the general human misery. These are, of course, pure science and technology. But the first is for Man the Abstract Thinker and the second for Man the Maker. It also seems to me that the English people are not subject to the very modern *furor technologicus* to the extent that the Russians and the Americans are. Even France, *mère des arts, des armes, et des lois,* is now creating a technological *mystique,* which is providing an emotional release for her people. The English people, though fully abreast of others in technological and scientific development, show no such enthusiasm. That perhaps is owing to the fact that they have been scientific discoverers for a long time and the pioneers of the technological revolution.

In any case, there is enough to give a sense of fulfilment to those men who live by and for science and technology. But for the men for whom the prophets, philosophers, and poets wrote in the past there are only catchwords. I do not think that there was any age in the past in which moral ideas were more powerless than in ours, when men are chattering ceaselessly about social and international morality. One can understand that. On the one hand, what feeble moral ideas we have are the remnants of the old humanitarianism which has lost its vitality and become obsolete. On the other, man's power has grown enormously and wholly outstripped his wisdom. The distance between the two can be judged by the pronouncements of the scientists themselves. Some of the worst platitudes of our times are coming from the discoverers of the mathematical equations and new laws of physics. These creators of new human power can do no better as moralists than cry like frightened children at the sight of the giant they have themselves brought into being.

This leaves to all Western nations, and Englishmen among them, only one thing to fall back on: their historic civilization. As soon as I came to this point in my thinking I also understood the real meaning of all that I had seen in England and France — the crowds at the classical plays, concerts, picture galleries, and exhibitions; the interest in architecture, gardens, and landscape; loyalty to religion and the *mos majorum;* the care bestowed on the interpretation and preservation of the national heritage; the love and piety inspired by all the aspects of the historic civilization, including even its politics.

I think their historic civilization has already become the ultimate resource of the existence of these peoples, though none of them has declared consciously like the Greeks of the Alexandrine age: 'Paideia is a haven for all mankind.' It is entering actively into their daily life to keep them steady and cheerful in situations which are full of disappointments and anxieties. Perhaps the power of the historic civilization is best seen in the effect it produces on the creators and preachers of contemporary culture. As soon as they turn their face from the present to the past they are restored to sanity, good sense, and sincerity. They recover humility and love. None of them dream of repeating in regard to Shakespeare or Michelangelo what they say about their own products. The attitudinizers become lovable personalities again.

Englishmen, it seems to me, are showing all the greater affection for the products of their historic civilization because they have become half-conscious of a peculiar neglect of them in the past. In England civilization has most often been identified with the art of living—literature, painting, architecture, and the other creations being looked upon as mere accessories. It was an English scholar who said that the last product of study was, not the book, but the man. The nation as a whole have thought the same thing about their civilization. They still think so, but they have also become aware that their civilized life is going to be endangered unless they re-orient their attitude, because they can no longer practise the art of living in the old manner. They must now fix their love on the permanent things, and put less trust in the evanescent style of living.

Yet this falling back on civilization is not *escape* for them, no retirement into the ivory tower, itself a catchword invented by those who love to sit on their handful of thorns to air their grievance against those who have the capacity to make themselves happy in the worst of circumstances. On the contrary, it appears to me that the only outlet that our age has to offer to the fighting spirit without which a man is a very poor creature, is to be found in the sphere of civilization. All other wars, even religious ones, have become inconceivable or immoral, and climbing Everest or reaching the Pole is not an adequate substitute. But the joy of combat is yet to be found in the war between civilization and the new democratic culture.

I do not understand why many intellectuals, who are watching this conflict and are conscious of the tremendous issues which hang on its outcome, are so pessimistic and depressed about it. Certainly, if absolute numbers of the followers of civilization are considered, they are more numerous today than at any time in the past. Greater numbers are enjoying good music and literature, taking an interest in architecture, painting and sculpture, and wanting to share the refinements of life. The credit for this has to go to the men of faith, courage, and energy who are interpreting and popularizing the historic civilization among the people. The movement of reclamation and conversion is strong, and it will continue to gain ground.

But, of course, the pity is that the new democratic culture is also gaining ground, and at a higher rate. It is recruiting ever greater numbers of followers in the old world of folk civilization which it has almost destroyed. It is not so much the appearance of the new culture as its inroads into folk civilization that are creating the greatest danger for civilization. The old folk culture was of the same stuff as the civilization, only simpler, the new culture is antithetical.

A greater danger lies in the political power behind the new culture. Perhaps for the first time in the history of mankind an ordinary majority has been put in a position of authority over an exceptional minority, with disastrous consequences for everything coming from the mind. This majority is conscious of its power, and is therefore also aggressive. There is a hard fight before civilization, and nobody can predict the result.

But that is no reason for losing heart. In any case, I found no defeatism in the rank and file of the new followers of civilization. Perhaps for the future more is to be expected from this Young Guard than the tired Old Guard. These men and women seemed not only to enjoy the historic civilization with immense zest in their own lives, they appeared also to be marching to battle to the tune of a brave music:

MARCHE DES DAVIDSBÜNDLER CONTRE LES PHILISTINS.

VII

NATIONAL DESTINY

IT MUST NOT BE imagined that I was free from doubts and misgivings all the time I was in England or did not wonder whether beneath the appearances everything was sound. As a matter of fact, I put to myself the most fundamental question of all, 'What was their national destiny?' That must sound pompous, but I shall explain what I had in mind. I was seeing a people who were going about their business with energy and confidence, who looked strong and healthy, had plenty of food and the other necessities of life, were even enjoying luxuries of which, living in India, I could form no idea, and altogether showed no signs of being tired or discouraged. To what was all this leading them as a nation? They had lost their Empire, the greater part of their wealth, also their position as the first World Power. Were they going to recover their old position, or create a new position of which they could be as proud, or were they, in spite of all their apparent recovery and prosperity, going down the path of inevitable decline? On account of my love for the English people I put these questions to myself. I also tried to find out if they were doing so themselves.

One day I asked an English friend whether there was any thinking on the national destiny among his people. I meant hard and objective thinking as distinct from hoping and generally feeling confident that things would turn out for the best. He immediately replied that there was no such thinking. 'We are wholly absorbed in the present,' he added. He seemed to imply that with his people it was a case of thinking that sufficient unto the day was, not the evil, but the good thereof.

But the question did not leave my mind. I went on thinking about it, and raised it once again when I was in Rome. My English friends there asked me if I had liked what I had seen in England. I replied that I had been very deeply impressed, but that it seemed to me as if they were thoughtless about the future. My hostess, to whom I repeated the formula about the national destiny, considered for a little while and said, 'You see, Mr Chaudhuri, we have had very bad times and we have come through, though we hardly knew how to. We have also recovered more rapidly than we could have believed to be possible. I think that is why we are enjoying the present for a little while. I am sure we are not really thoughtless about the future.' I felt reassured.

The question has returned to my mind, but not in the old form. I still feel uncertain about the future, and I believe it is impossible to say anything definite about it at this stage. But I have no criticism to make of the present attitude of the English people and I withdraw every suggestion of blame which was implied in my question. I now think that they are wholly right in going about as they are doing, making the best of their imperishable resources of happiness and showing a brave thoughtlessness as regards their troubles.

It is unnecessary to give more thought to them than they deserve. For the English people there is no longer any question of going forward to meet a challenge like that of 1940. If they have to face a situation in the future which will be a matter of life and death for them, it will not come through their own will but that of others, and all that will be needed then will be stoical endurance. It will not be called 'their finest hour'.

Their worst troubles are with them, and they are here and now. They are of such a kind that heroism lies in not paying any attention to them and going about one's work and amusements as if nothing was wrong. I cannot say that the English people have risen wholly above their present troubles, for they do show at times an irritation and moodiness which is more serious than the national habit of grumbling. But I am surprised and delighted to see them as happy, careless, and gay as they generally are. And the most delightful thing is that they do not even have the cleverness to say: '*Il faut cultiver notre jardin.*'

But when in England I had no perception of all this or of

the relationship between their contemporary situation and their historic civilization. I could only see the richness and strength of their ultimate resources, and how accessible these were. This by itself was a great joy to me, and I told everybody that never before, except in the intimacy of my family life, had I been so happy as I was during my short stay in England. It was the literal truth, and the happiness has lasted.

At the beginning it was overflowing, and I myself became conscious that I was wearing my joy on my sleeve. But there was good reason to be swept off the platform of cool sense. My experiences in England were followed by no less remarkable ones in Paris and Rome, and in the end they all became as happily fused as are the main subject, foreground, and background in a well-composed picture.

I cannot describe my sightseeing in Paris and Rome in this book, but just to indicate the nature of my experiences I shall say something about the last hours of my stay in Europe. After I had brought down my luggage to the hall of the hotel I thought I would go and sit on the Capitol, which I had seen in the evening of the day of my arrival. So I went up the magnificent steps, and wandered around in Michelangelo's Campidoglio, the garden on the side above Mamertine Prison, and the park on the opposite side above the Tarpeian Rock, where once stood the Temple of Jupiter Capitolinus. I also sat for some time at the foot of the statue of Marcus Aurelius and in the church of Santa Maria in Aracoeli.

I recalled that Gibbon had sat somewhere near by and conceived the idea of writing his great history, as he mused amidst the ruins of the Capitol. But just to recollect the incident was all that I could do at the moment. I had become as incapable of moralizing in the humanistic vein as of feeling the poetry of ruins in the romantic manner. It was the vision before my eyes that was absorbing all my attention.

The famous golden light of Rome was losing its gold and turning into grey. The Via Cavour in the distance could be seen glittering with its shop-lights, and Santa Maria Maggiore loomed above it. Before me the three arches of the Basilica of Maxentius looked like the mouths of vast primitive caverns, shaped into symmetry by the Roman notion of order. The ruins of the

Forum were falling under the deep shadows cast by the green mass of the Palatine.

But Rome has adopted a most effective method of displaying her ruins. Suddenly, unseen floodlights were switched on, and the buildings began to gleam like the figures of cameos against their background. As it grew darker and darker, they became brighter and brighter, until the Arches of Severus and Titus, the columns of the Temples of Vespasian and Saturn, the three shafts of the Temple of Castor and Pollux with their entablature, even the little Temple of Vesta which had been recently restored, shone like fragments of architecture quarried out of the full moon. The Colosseum, which appears so menacingly solid and sombre in the daytime, seemed to have lost all its weight and become aerial.

In London I had already seen the facade of Somerset House and the dome of St Paul's illuminated at night. In Paris the floodlit dome of the Invalides was a lovely vision which I saw every evening through my hotel window. But I had never come across anything more beautiful and moving than the phosphorescent ruins of the Roman Forum.

The excitement of these experiences must have passed into my movements, for when three hours later I got into the aeroplane at Ciampino I noticed a fellow-passenger, obviously an Englishman, watching me with an amused smile. I wondered what oddity in my appearance or behaviour was making him do so. The mystery was cleared up at Baghdad.

When we were waiting in the hall of the airport, he came forward and introduced himself as an Englishman in the business line who had lived for many years in Calcutta. When I said I was a Bengali he replied that he had never seen a Bengali like me. Then turning to the air hostess he observed, 'Is he not bubbling over with life?' I answered with an affectation of English ways, 'Oh, that's nothing. I've just had a holiday at the expense of your country and France!' They both laughed. But it was useless to pretend. My happiness was flowing out of very much deeper springs.

THE END